DIALOGUES
IN METAPSYCHIATRY

DIALOGUES IN METAPSYCHIATRY

THOMAS HORA

A Crossroad Book

THE SEABURY PRESS : NEW YORK

1977   :   The Seabury Press   :   815 Second Avenue   :   New York, N.Y. 10017

Printed in the United States of America
Library of Congress Cataloging in Publication Data

Hora, Thomas.
  Dialogues in metapsychiatry.

  "A Crossroad book."
  Bibliography: p.
  1. Conduct of life.   I. Title.
BJ1581.2.H64   170'.202   77–8268
ISBN 0–8164–0352–X

. . . this is life eternal,
that they might know thee the
only true God,
and Jesus Christ,
whom thou hast sent.

John 17:3

The meaning
and purpose of life
is to come to know
Reality.

To the seekers
and the knockers
and the askers,
in gratitude.
For the seeker
and the finder
are one in Love.

CONTENTS

CONTENTS

DIALOGUES
IN METAPSYCHIATRY

PREFACE

It seems advisable to explain right from the beginning what this book is not. First of all, this is not a religious book, neither is it a non-religious book. Second, it is not just another book on group psychotherapy, even though it may seem so at first to many who may read it.

The frequent Biblical references are used here as fundamental statements about the nature of existential reality and a means of realizing a transcendence of the human condition, which is seen as cognitively underdeveloped.

Existential metapsychiatry is a scientific method of healing and education based on metaphysical concepts of man and the universe. Man is here understood to be an "image and likeness of God," or preferably, a manifestation of cosmic Love-Intelligence. He is assumed to be capable of attaining higher levels of consciousness and of beholding reality in its spiritual dimension. While traditional methods of group psychotherapy tend to be psychological, interactional, interpersonal, psychoanalytic, or of the encounter type, the "metagroup" is essentially hermeneutic. By this is meant that the central focus is the elucidation of the *truth of being.*

The participants are engaged in a joint venture of seeking to understand their lives in an existentially valid way. The right understanding of what is existentially valid brings man into harmony with the fundamental order of being. This, in turn, results in healing and transformation of character.

The principles of existential metapsychiatry have been described in a more systematic way in the preceding book (*Existential Metapsychiatry*, The Seabury Press). However, much can be gained just by patiently immersing oneself in the dialogic interchange as it is described in the following pages.

Dialogue No. 1

THE SUPREME WAY

Question: I would like to know the meaning of two experiences which occurred recently. About three weeks ago, while driving on the road, a pheasant flew out of a bush and crashed into my car, it literally attacked the car. And last weekend, as I was driving, a car smashed into me from behind. Again it seemed that I was being attacked.

Dr. Hora: As you know, nothing comes into our experience uninvited. We are never involuntary victims. What is the difference between being attacked and receiving compliments?

Comment: One feels bad and one feels good.

Comment: A kick is as good as a boost.

Dr. Hora: Right. Isn't it dangerous to desire compliments?

Comment: Yes.

Dr. Hora: It is very dangerous. Do you desire compliments?

Comment: I like them, but I also feel uneasy when they come.

Dr. Hora: The desire for praise, admiration, recognition, compliments, all invite the possibility of attacks, physical or mental. Often we don't realize how we are inviting trouble. In one of our groups there is a lovely young lady who was walking one day in front of the Museum of Natural History and a man came over to her, grabbed her by the neck, and said to her, "Woman, get ready to die!" And then he spat in her face, threw her down to the ground, and walked away. Being quite enlightened, she said to herself, "Thanks, I needed that." Immediately she knew that it had been invited.

We have to be sufficiently enlightened to know that we are not born for the purpose of getting compliments and gold stars and kicks in the pants. We are not here to be targets. It is important to know who we are, what we are, and what our purpose in life is. There are only two ways to become a victim: by wanting to or by not wanting to, by being attractive or by being unattractive.

Comment: The ego must die.

Dr. Hora: Yes.

Comment: To follow up my story about the car, in order to get to work, I had to borrow my friend's car. I parked it in front of the house, and next morning I found the front tire flat. Is this just more of the same?

Dr. Hora: Well, maybe it is time to discover who you really are and what your purpose in life is.

Comment: You once told us a story about a student of Zen who was given a drawing to meditate on. The drawing consisted of a circle with a dot in the center. After some years of meditation, the student realized that he had to erase the circle. Later he realized that he also had to erase the dot. And at that point he became enlightened. Now my question is, who erased the dot?

Comment: There was no dot in the first place; therefore, no one erased it.

Dr. Hora: That's a somewhat intellectual answer.

Comment: Understanding erased it.

Dr. Hora: Right. How can understanding erase the circle and the dot? Does understanding have an eraser?

Comment: Yes, it erases appearances and false beliefs.

Dr. Hora: What does "understanding erases appearances and false beliefs" mean?

Comment: It means that appearances have nothing to hang onto any more. Appearances seem to cling to certain false beliefs that we cherish.

Dr. Hora: Remember the story I once told you about two people who came into a living room? One got panicky because he saw a rat in the middle of the room. The other was calm; he saw a dry oak leaf. Who changed the rat into an oak leaf?

Comment: Right seeing.

Dr. Hora: Right seeing erases misperceptions of what really is. When someone is getting hit by a pheasant—or a peasant —and getting into accidents, it indicates that he is misperceiving himself as an individual in this world. He sees himself as an individual who is either attractive or unattractive and who needs compliments or persecutions, praise, pity and pampering. This is where the trouble lies. We misperceive ourselves and we misperceive others; we misperceive reality and suffer the consequences. As we seek enlightenment, we pray, "Open thou mine eyes that I may see better." And as we improve our ability to see—as God improves it—then what previously appeared to be a rat is suddenly just an oak leaf. We see things according to the way they really are. And our troubles are healed, they disappear. The tires don't go flat, people don't smash into us, things tend to work together for good. It is not because God is pleased and is rewarding us for having behaved better. It is not a reward, even though it is rewarding to be enlightened. The good of God is not a reward. God does not work on a merit system.

Question: What is God?

Dr. Hora: You don't know?

Comment: I may have some idea or concept of God, but it may not be correct. If I can come to a point of understanding that the idea of the self dies, then God would reveal itself. Do I need to know what God is or would it just manifest itself? Then there wouldn't be a self looking at God, there would be just One.

Dr. Hora: This is an argument which the Hindus and the Buddhists frequently raise. They say, "All you have to do is to achieve emptiness in meditation and then you will know everything. It is not good to have a concept of God." Well, to have a concept of God can be bad. On the other hand, it can be very good.

Comment: That sounds ridiculous.

Dr. Hora: Right. You don't understand it?

Comment: Yes, I understand it.

Dr. Hora: Then tell us.

Comment: I don't know how to explain it. So if it is the right concept, then it is good and helpful.

Dr. Hora: What is the right concept?

Comment: If God is Principle.

Dr. Hora: That's right. Many good Christians and Jews have a concept of God, but that concept becomes a stumbling block in their progress toward enlightenment, because any concept of God which can be imagined is the wrong concept. If we can imagine what God is, we are only religious.

Question: Can a principle be imagined?

Dr. Hora: No, it can only be understood. So if our concept of God can be imagined, then we are in trouble. This will then interfere with enlightenment.

Question: But even if God is Principle, isn't there a separation between God and man?

Dr. Hora: All right, so we admit that to have a concept of God can be a great stumbling block to enlightenment. What happens if we follow the Buddhist recommendation of no concept of God at all and just seek enlightenment through emptiness? What happens then?

Comment: It seems as if you are negating everything and chasing after some kind of a ghost.

Comment: Last weekend we were listening to an Indian guru; he said that meditation is the silence between two thoughts and that in this silence God can reveal himself.

Dr. Hora: It could be, but it also has its pitfalls. Just as Western man has his pitfalls in conceptual thinking and imagination, the Oriental approach has the pitfalls of nihilism.

Comment: Emptiness just doesn't exist.

Dr. Hora: Emptiness can also become an imagined concept. The supreme teacher and greatest master is Jesus Christ. He taught in riddles and parables, through demonstration and example. He gave us the approach which is neither Western nor Eastern, but just right. The Bible says: "The weapons of our warfare are not carnal but mighty through God to the pulling down of strongholds; casting down imaginations and every high thing that exalteth itself against the knowledge of God, and bringing into captivity every thought to the obedience of Christ" (II Corinthians 10: 4,5).

This is the method which is neither Eastern nor Western. What kind of a method is it? It is an epistemological method. What do we mean by that? It leads us in the direction of discovering true knowledge. Knowledge which is neither conceptual nor nonconceptual but is a realization of our oneness with divine Mind, and it teaches us how to have that mind which was also in Christ Jesus. When it says, ". . . bringing into captivity every thought to the obedience of Christ . . ." it means attaining that consciousness where our thoughts come to us from the divine Mind all the time and not from the filing cabinet, a continual flow of inspiration. This, of course, is a protection against Oriental nihilism.

Question: What does that mean?

Dr. Hora: In the search for emptiness there is a danger of becoming completely negative, apathetic, passive, appreciating nothing in this world, and losing a sense of usefulness. We can spend six or nine hours sitting cross-legged staring at a blank wall until we become stultified, and nothing will happen and we are nowhere. And we can do it for years, wasting our lives and contributing nothing.

Comment: I have opened up the Bible today and read that Jesus said to his disciples, "Go ye into all the world, and preach the gospel to every creature" (Mark 16:15). Also, "Heal the sick, cleanse the lepers, raise the dead, cast out devils . . ." (Matthew 10:8). This indicates to me that his way was a very constructive and positive mode of being-in-the-world.

Dr. Hora: He did not tell them to sit cross-legged and do nothing, or to go out and seek popularity by attracting compliments or attacks, making friends and influencing people.

Comment: When I take out the Bible and try to meditate, I experience fear.

Dr. Hora: Some people do experience fear at this point. What is this fear?

Comment: I think we fear giving up something that we cherish.

Comment: The ego.

Dr. Hora: Personal existence is something that we know. Spiritual existence is something we don't know.

Comment: It seems to me that what was being asked was: "Is there a self after enlightenment or is there nothing, just the undifferentiated aesthetic continuum?" I think I heard it explained that there is individual consciousness. Is that true?

Comment: What you just said is very helpful. I am interested, but I don't know what else there is. But I am looking forward to the joy which I have glimpsed in meditation. I would like to know more about this individual consciousness, what it really is.

Dr. Hora: Have you ever heard of PAGL (peace, assurance, gratitude, and love)? Have you ever been amazed by the wisdom that came out of your mouth unexpectedly? That's what it is. Imagine if one could always be such a channel for wisdom, love, peace, assurance, joy, harmony, and if all things around us could be beautiful and good and prosperous.

There is another danger with the Oriental approach, namely, to settle for poverty. One bowl of rice a day, a saffron robe, and no shoes—and this would become a virtue to be proud of. There are many pitfalls, both in Eastern as well as in the Western approaches and, as Jesus said, "Wide is the gate, and broad is the way, that leadeth to destruction, and many there be which go in thereat: Because strait is the gate, and narrow is the way, which leadeth unto life, and few there be that find it" (Matthew 7:13,14).

Question: How could one retain the things one learns here? I seem to understand everything, it makes so much sense. But when I go home, I lose it all.

Dr. Hora: It is a mistake to try to retain what is being said here. It is not to be kept in a filing cabinet; maybe that's the problem.

Comment: What is needed is to be able to hear the ideas.

Dialogue No. 2

THE PERFECT PRINCIPLE

Question: What does it mean to let God help us?

Dr. Hora: As long as we are involved with futile questions such as: 1. What's wrong? 2. How do you feel? 3. Why? 4. Who is to blame? 5. What should I do? 6. How should I do it?, we are not letting God help us. It is most amazing, if we consider it, that man seems to be able to foil God. We can seemingly foil God by dwelling in the structure of thought revolving around the above questions. In the light of this discovery, effective living boils down to one single principle, namely, learning to let God do his work in our lives. Learning how not to interfere with the good of God expressing itself in us and through us.

When aviation was developing, engineers began to study the principles of aerodynamics. Most people never knew that there were principles of aerodynamics—some don't know it even today—but they discovered that certain shapes of wings, when put into a wind tunnel, would reveal the existence of certain principles which were called aerodynamic principles. And it has been observed that the wind behaves in a certain way according to the shape of the wing. For millions of years no one knew about this, and then they were able to construct a wing in such a way as to reveal in a most perfect manner the principles of aerodynamics. It was there all the time; but until that particular shape, called the airfoil, was designed, the precise nature of the principles was not known, it was not possible to know them. But now they are known and can be mathematically formulated, and this is a law which is as clear as the fact that two and two is four. And so it is with God.

What is God? God too is a principle, a principle of perfect life. People do not understand it, and they cannot even imagine that it could be possible for man to understand the principle of perfect life, just as it was not known that a perfect plane could be designed in accordance with the principles of aerodynamics. Now if we were to tell someone that the futile questions violate the principle of perfect Love-Intelligence, that they make it impossible for man to realize perfect life, he would be very skeptical and say that there is no such thing, and that everybody knows that these questions are very practical and necessary and all intelligent people are asking them.

The more we understand the principle of perfect harmony and love and intelligence, the more we come to realize that learning to ask right questions can bring us into harmony with the God-Principle and improve our "flying." As we come to understand the answers to intelligent questions we are brought into harmony with the principle which is God and we partake in the blessings of God's goodness, and move through life with a minimum of turbulence.

Comment: And with the greatest amount of uplift.

Dr. Hora: Jesus said, "Be ye therefore perfect, even as your Father which is in heaven is perfect" (Matthew 5:48). We had to find the perfect shape for a wing—the airfoil—in order to discover the perfect law of aerodynamics, so we want to find the perfect answer to the perfect principle of life. The whole idea that God is a principle is a revolutionary idea.

Question: What is it that corresponds in the realm of life to the airfoil?

Dr. Hora: The two valid questions: "What is the meaning of what seems to be?" and "What is what really *is?*"

Question: Is asking these questions a form of prayer?

Dr. Hora: Certainly. The two perfect questions are an approach to the perfect prayer. What is perfect prayer?

Comment: Beholding.

Dr. Hora: Beholding. In aviation technology beholding has been made easier with the help of the wind tunnel. In existential studies how can we improve our ability to behold? By demonstrating in individual experience the perfect life, which is characterized by PAGL. When an airplane is designed in correspondence to the perfect principles of aerodynamics, it glides perfectly, securely, swiftly, harmoniously. And so when we are in harmony with the God principle, we are aware of peace, assurance, gratitude, and love.

When we are confronted with some crisis, emergency, or problem, it requires quite a bit of devotion to refrain from asking the futile (invalid) questions and start asking, "What is the meaning of what seems to be?" And then proceed with the most perfect question: "What is what really *is?*"

Question: If we ask the first valid question, will that reveal the error in our thought?

Dr. Hora: Yes, if we really want to know. But we do not always want to know. You see, the invalid questions came into being as an evasion of facing up to what really needs to be known. We don't really want to know because it is often embarrassing. But if we are willing to be embarrassed, the answer will reveal itself to us. And we shall be rewarded by being able to find the answer to the final question.

Question: Where do meanings come from?

Dr. Hora: Meanings of problems have a common denominator which is self-confirmatory ideation.

Question: Can God be imagined?

Dr. Hora: The most prevailing idea of God is that he is some faraway personage, that man has to somehow reach out to him, that prayer is the way of reaching him, and that man is here and God is there. Religious dogma speaks of the Holy Other; God is the Holy Other. But Jesus said that God and man are one, inseparable. Just as a sunbeam does not have to move toward the sun—it moves away from the sun without ever losing contact with it—so man is an emanation of God without ever losing contact with God. "I and my Father are one" (John 10:30). "I am in the Father, and the Father in me" (John 14:11).

When we pray we are not trying to reach God with our prayers. What are we trying to achieve? We are trying to realize that we are emanating from God and therefore we are partaking in all the qualities of God. Now this is a radical difference, and I hope you can appreciate it because it is also very revolutionary. We do not pray to God, we pray to realize that we are emanations of God.

Comment: That's the meaning of the question, "What is what really *is?*"

Dr. Hora: Right. The idea of man having to reach to God in prayer is a very widespread and deeply ingrained erroneous assumption. The important thing is that we do not move toward God; we are emanating from God. When we come to understand and see ourselves as emanations of divine Principle, then it is very easy for us to understand that we are Godlike. That which emanates from God has all the qualities of God. The sunbeam emanating from the sun has all the qualities of the sun. We are all radiances of Love-Intelligence. We are always at one with God. We never have to establish contact with God, and this radical difference changes our mode of prayer.

Question: What is the right way to understand the phrase "Our Father who art in heaven"?

Dr. Hora: We are with him in heaven for we are emanations of him.

Question: Are you saying that along with all the qualities of God we have all the power of God?

Dr. Hora: Sure.

Question: We have the power to create rivers and move mountains?

Dr. Hora: The power which we express is not our power. The source of all power and life and intelligence is God and is God's. Jesus, who understood his oneness with his divine source more than anyone else who ever lived, has demonstrated fantastic powers. He raised the dead and instantly healed people who were crippled for many years. And it was the power of God manifested through him. We are constantly making progress, divine intelligence is reaching the world and expressing itself through man. And we see all sorts of marvels.

Question: Dr. Hora, what is life?

Dr. Hora: It is an essential quality of God, just like love, intelligence, power, creativity, and perfection. These are all attributes of the God principle. But above all, I would like you to achieve a shift of perspective when it comes to prayer.

When we are praying we are not trying to climb up to God, we are trying to realize that we are emanations from God. If a wave were praying, it wouldn't try to reach the ocean; the wave would try to realize that it is inseparable from the ocean. That is a tremendous difference which helps us gain a more perfect understanding of the principle of God and man. We don't really have a relationship to God or with God, we have an at-one-ment with God.

Suppose an individual has a headache and he becomes conscious of the fact that he is an emanation of God. Then he can ask himself, "Does God have a headache? Could I, being an emanation of God, have anything that God doesn't have?" In that moment the headache must go. Only God's qualities constitute our being. Whatever we seem to be having that God does not have, we don't really have, and is not legitimate. The more ignorant we are of the true situation which exists between God and man, the more effectively we can fool ourselves and vice versa. The more clearly we can understand ourselves to be emanations of God, the more impossible it is for us to be in pain, to be aggressive, to be jealous, to be mean, to be unloving, to be fearful, to be greedy, to be stupid, because God is none of these things. We shall see clearly that only divine qualities constitute our true being.

Now we are learning the prayer of beholding, and we said we have to behold ourselves in the context of divine reality. We can go a step further, we can behold ourselves and others as emanations of the divine Godhead. What's a Godhead? It is the divine source of all that really is.

Question: Can we consider source outside of time and space?

Dr. Hora: In divine reality there is no time and space. We are timeless, immortal. Space is just a human illusion, and so is time. God knows nothing about it.

Comment: I am trying to see emanation outside of the context of time and space.

Dr. Hora: If you see emanation outside the context of time and space, then you are dividing reality into two parts: one where there is time and space and another where there is no time and space. Reality is one, unreality is not. Divine reality is the only reality that really is. Prayer is an endeavor to come to realize what really is. If we learn to pray in this manner, we shall be greatly blessed by our contact with the truth of what really is. Then we shall come to know the truth increasingly well and this truth will bless us, heal us, and liberate us from problems that seem to be.

In the realm of the real there are no problems, there is only perfect being. We experience problems. Now let us put it this way, problems are not realities, they are experiences. Nothing comes into experience uninvited. Can you conceive yourselves as emanations of God? Can anyone? The practical implication of this is that we can separate ourselves from whatever is not perfect, and we can identify ourselves with everything that is beautiful and wholesome and good and loving. These are divine, and only the divine qualities in us constitute our being.

Dialogue No. 3

THE REAL

Question: Is self-indulgence harmful?

Comment: The word "self" leaves God out of the picture.

Dr. Hora: Aren't there many happy atheists in the world who seem to be prosperous and having a good time? Let us clarify the difference between religion and what we are talking about here. Religion is essentially based on a "should" system and a "thou shalt not" system. It is set up in such a way that there is a divine authority over man, and this authority makes certain demands on man. There are rules for behavior and many prohibitions. If we look at it this way, we see a regimentation program. There is a divine authority which is regimenting our lives. Essentially, we live in fear. We obey or disobey. If we obey, we resent it; if we disobey, we are afraid of punishment. Of course this is all very childish. There is no such God, we don't have a master-slave relationship with a divine authority who is overseeing us and forcing us to renounce certain pleasures in order to please him, or to behave in a certain way to please him and hope that we will be rewarded. Someone remarked that the superego feels good when everything else in us feels bad.

It is important to know the difference between religion and reality. We can live on the basis of obedience to a divine authority, or a system of ethics, or a system of intimidation, or we can live on the basis of understanding what really is. And that is the difference between being religious and being enlightened. There are some people who obey traffic regulations, stop at red lights, keep to the right, observe every rule, and are quite good drivers. But they do it out of fear of being caught by the police. One can be a good driver out of fear or one can be a good driver on the basis of understanding and a higher appreciation of traffic regulations as a civilized system of communication and transportation. When we are afraid, we are religious. But the real God is pure Love-Intelligence. And the Bible says, "There is no fear in love; but perfect love casteth out fear" (I John 4:18).

Let us consider the issue of self-indulgence. Most people get upset if they are discouraged from indulging themselves. If we take a bone away from a dog, he will growl at us because we are depriving him of his self-indulgent pleasure. If we interfere with the pleasurable pursuits of an unenlightened man, he too will get angry. However, if we come to realize that self-indulgence is existentially invalid, then we are not talking about a God who is a killjoy, we are talking about the nature of perfect reality.

Now what could be better than pleasure? This is an issue which we must come to terms with sooner or later. Self-indulgence, vanity, pride, and ambition are very difficult—actually impossible—to give up. Religion does not try to liberate us from these human afflictions, religion tries to discipline us against them and get us to control ourselves. If we are ambitious, let's not be so ambitious; if we are vain, let's not look in the mirror so much; if we are proud, let's temper our bragging and showing off; if we are self-indulgent, let's be moderate. This is hard to do. Of course, moderating or controlling is not going to increase our freedom, it will diminish it and we will live in a constant undercurrent of conflict. There will always be a certain amount of friction—like the good schoolchildren who sit quietly but who would like to scream. So religion does not liberate, it merely controls. But there is a way to be liberated, although it is not an easy matter. What is required for liberation?

Comment: Being interested in understanding the true nature of existence and appreciating it.

Dr. Hora: Some religions, having discovered that self-indulgence is not good, have recommended asceticism. What is asceticism?

Comment: Self-indulgence.

Dr. Hora: It is the opposite of self-indulgence.

Comment: But it is still concerned with the self.

Dr. Hora: Yes, but it doesn't feel good. Wouldn't that make God happy? Instead of making ourselves feel good, we make ourselves feel bad. The age-old fallacy is this: if God looks with disdain on self-indulgence then it will probably please him if we inflict suffering on ourselves. In India people are piercing themselves with needles and walking on fire and doing all sorts of things to propitiate the divine authority which looks with disfavor on feeling good.

What is our premise here? God is not a person. What is God? God is an *is*. What's an *is?* The Bible says, "For he maketh his sun to rise on the evil and on the good, and sendeth rain on the just and on the unjust" (Matthew 5:45). Now is that fair? From a religious standpoint it would seem unfair. So we must go beyond popular traditional ideas about religiosity. Religiosity does not solve anything. Perhaps it makes people behave themselves in a little more civilized manner. What is important is to be liberated from the universal desire for self-confirmatory thinking. In what way is feeling good self-confirmatory thinking? The trouble with self-indulgence is not that we are indulging ourselves with the good or the pleasurable; it is the thoughts which underlie the experience that constitute the problem. Self-indulgence or vanity or pride or ambition or shame or embarrassment or slothfulness are all varieties of one theme: I-me. That is, self-confirmatory ideation.

Question: How do we turn away from this?

Dr. Hora: This is a valid question. But an even more valid question would be: What else is there? What else is there besides self-confirmatory ideation? Well, you could say, we could think of others and be altruistic. That is an ethical solution to the problem of self-confirmatory thinking. But ethics, based on human reasoning, are not helpful because they are not based on a valid perception of reality. To be unselfish is no different from being selfish. If we are altruistic, our thinking is still personal and horizontal and shallow. One can be unselfish for selfish reasons. So altruism, while it sounds nice within the context of ethical reasoning, is essentially not valid. "For the good that I would I do not; but the evil which I would not, that I do" (Romans 7:19).

Ordinary human reasoning, unenlightened human reasoning, can be compared to a line. It is narrow, it is horizontal, it is shallow, it is linear. But reality is not a line, it is a sphere. The thinking of unenlightened man compares to the thinking of enlightened man as a line compares to a sphere. A line is one-dimensional; a sphere is full-dimensional. What is required of us to break out from one-dimensional thinking? What is it that determines our thought processes? What makes unenlightened man a shallow, one-dimensional, horizontal, narrow-minded thinker? It seems logical to think that way because things just look like that. Common sense tells us that there is me and there is you and there is nothing else. So if we judge by appearances, it is logical, commonsensical, rational, natural to think in a one-dimensional way. "As thou seest, so thou beest." When we rely on our sensory perceptions alone, it is inevitable for us to become one-dimensional thinkers. And out of this flow all the various problems we touched upon, especially self-confirmatory thinking.

Every problem we run into in life is based on judging reality by how it looks. Now what are the five gates of hell? Sensualism, emotionalism, intellectualism, materialism, and personalism. What are these based on? They are based on sensory perception. The five gates of hell are based on judging reality as it appears to be and having no idea of how it really is. Cause-and-effect thinking is part and parcel of this complex of narrow-minded, shallow, linear thinking. It is not easy to rise above cause-and-effect thinking. We have to struggle against the futile questions. When we are natural and logical or rationalistic, we are in trouble. Liberation stems from becoming increasingly capable of being aware of what really is. When we are aware of what really is, then there is no problem with self-indulgence or non-self-indulgence, or vanity or pride or ambition.

Dialogue No. 4

THE RIGHT CONTEXT

Question: I am faced with a dilemma: whether I should join people at lunchtime or eat by myself. On weekends I don't know whether I should call somebody and socialize or stay by myself and meditate—which, of course, I don't do.

Dr. Hora: In other words, you don't know what you *should* do.

Comment: Sometimes socializing is just using someone else for entertainment. I know that this is wrong; but then I wonder if it is ever valid to socialize.

Comment: I am quite aware of the fact that using people is wrong, but when I am alone I daydream, or I can do all sorts of things that are not valid—masturbate, for instance. It is no solution not to be with people.

Dr. Hora: What is the real problem here?

Comment: The real problem is "should" thinking.

Dr. Hora: Just because the vast majority of people are in the habit of asking certain questions, it does not mean that these questions are valid or helpful. As a matter of fact, they tend to sidetrack our thought processes into channels where there are no solutions. Should I socialize or shouldn't I socialize? This is a question for Emily Post. The wrong questions appear to be right questions because other people are asking them too; but we need to know how to ask intelligent questions. Then we shall find answers and we will be able to live intelligently. What makes the above question a futile question?

Comment: She is asking this of herself, she is not looking beyond herself for answers.

Dr. Hora: Yes. The invalid questions put us into an invalid context. The context of the ego. The idea behind it is that man is a self-existent personage whose being in the world depends on personal decisions and choices. There are no such people really, they just seem to be. Man does not live in the context of his ego. Where does man live? He lives in divine reality. We are not concerned with social etiquette, we are concerned with existential issues and what constitutes intelligent living. Emily Post would say that intelligent living consists of socializing, having many friends, influencing many people, and doing all the things that one should do.

Comment: Not only Emily Post, but the whole world shouts this idea.

Dr. Hora: But it doesn't really solve anything; it just complicates life. How important it is to avoid asking the wrong questions and to know how to ask the right questions! Can anyone here ask the right question and get into the right context in which to view yourself? Do enlightened people socialize? Are they antisocial?

Comment: They neither socialize nor are they antisocial. I would say they are about the Father's business.

Dr. Hora: What does that mean at lunchtime in the cafeteria?

Comment: To be receptive to guidance which comes from the real source.

Dr. Hora: Could you speak English?

Comment: Sometimes it is good to ask oneself what would be the most loving response to a situation.

Dr. Hora: When in doubt ask, "Who am I? What is life? What does God want? What is needed?" Do these questions make sense? Can we answer these questions for all of us?

Comment: It certainly expands the question from "What is the most loving thing to do?" to "Who is it that is being loving?" It takes it beyond the person.

Dr. Hora: The answer is: I am a manifestation of Love-Intelligence. Life is God. What does life want? Life wants to be manifested. God wants us to shine in the cafeteria, in the street, at the desk, on the job, at a tea party; wherever we are it is always the same. If we ask the right questions, then we have no problems whatsoever; if we ask the wrong questions, then we are like fish out of water.

Comment: Then no matter what you do, it is wrong.

Dr. Hora: Right. If we socialize, we will be disappointed; if we refrain from socializing, we will be unhappy and lonely. We are damned if we do and damned if we don't. There is no answer in the context of the ego.

Comment: What surprises me is that you didn't talk about motives.

Dr. Hora: There is one healthy motive, namely, to be what one is. And that is the will of God, that we manifest the truth of being.

Question: Is motivation a sort of psychological term?

Dr. Hora: Right. Man cannot help but be the son of God.

Comment: If you see yourself as being apart from God, then motive is a very important factor.

Dr. Hora: Right. You are seeing yourself out of context, you are like a fish out of water. How long can a fish survive in the wrong environment? If we see ourselves in the world rather than in the context of divine reality, then things don't go well with us.

Here it would be appropriate to consider the issue of social pressures. People complain a great deal about social pressures. If we were to put "a piece of social pressure" under a microscope, so to speak, what would we find? We would find a big "should." What should be and what shouldn't be. And this is communicated either verbally or nonverbally. Can one be completely immune to social pressures? Is it possible?

Comment: Yes.

Dr. Hora: What is required to realize that possibility?

Comment: You really need to know that you are an instrument of God and that God is directing you. Then it would make no difference what other people expected, and you could always be loving and the "right man."

Dr. Hora: It also helps to know that we don't live in the world but in divine reality. The Bible puts it this way: "The law of the Spirit of life in Christ Jesus hath made me free from the law of sin and death" (Romans 8:2). When we understand that we live and move and have our being in divine reality, then the conventions and pressures and the "shoulds" and the "no-nos" of society do not apply to us. Does that mean that we become antisocial?

Comment: This reminds me of a time when I thought I had

to go to a school meeting because I thought I should. But then I decided I didn't feel like going. On the one hand, I was involved with should and shouldn't, that is, with social pressures; on the other hand, I was being antisocial and self-indulgent. I didn't care what social pressures were, I wanted to do what I felt like doing. I wasn't concerned about what is best, or what God wants. And I just realized it now, because in the past I would always be involved with one issue or the other.

Dr. Hora: That's a wonderful point. We can become antisocial if we substitute social demands for the demands of personal feelings, and then we are on a collision course with society. So that's not it. We don't live in our feelings and we don't live in the world. We live in the context of divine reality. And if we live in divine reality, we are neither conformists nor nonconformists. What are we?

Comment: Beneficial presences.

Dr. Hora: Does the Bible speak about being a conformist or a nonconformist?

Comment: "Be not conformed to this world: but be ye transformed by the renewing of your mind, that ye may prove what is that good, and acceptable, and perfect, will of God" (Romans 12:2).

Dr. Hora: That's living in divine reality. And then we shall have no problems, neither with ourselves nor with society. If we don't go to the meeting, nobody will miss us; if we go to the meeting, we are not going to miss out on anything.

Comment: We shouldn't have a personal preference whether to go or not to go.

Dr. Hora: We don't say what should be or what shouldn't be, we are concerned solely with what is. The best way to be blessed is to be a blessing. Learning to refrain from asking futile questions helps us to see ourselves in the right context. And what is enlightenment? Seeing what really is, rather than what people say it is.

Dialogue No. 5

THINKING AND KNOWING

Question: How can we lose our preconceived ideas about ourselves? For example, when I come here, my preconceived idea about myself is that of inadequacy, of asking wrong questions, of being judged. I keep saying to myself, well, I am a child of God, I am not inadequate. But still there is a sense of inadequacy. What can one do to overcome that?

Dr. Hora: There is nothing one can *do,* something needs to be *known.* However, this is an important question. Does anyone else have a preconceived idea about himself? Is there anyone who does *not* have a preconceived idea?

Comment: We have preconceived ideas about every facet of life.

Dr. Hora: Right. We are loaded with preconceived ideas about what should be and what shouldn't be.

Comment: If we could lose them, we could probably be perfectly healthy.

Dr. Hora: Whoever would lose his preconceived ideas about himself, would discover perfection, freedom, joy, love, intelligence, perspicacity, so on. Let us then face the fact that we are all hampered by preconceived ideas. Suppose someone has a preconceived idea that he is great. Is that good?

Comment: That is also not good.

Dr. Hora: So now the question is: "Can man be liberated from preconceived ideas about himself and others?" What do we call preconceived ideas about others?

Comment: Prejudice.

Dr. Hora: Right. So we are prejudiced against ourselves. Isn't that strange? And prejudiced against others. Jesus said, "Thou shalt love thy neighbor as thyself" (Matthew 19:19). He knew that prejudice is a two-edged sword. Love is a sword without a blade. What is the function of prejudice?

DIALOGUES IN METAPSYCHIATRY

Comment: It is judging by appearances.

Dr. Hora: Yes, but sometimes we are judging even before we have seen the appearance. If we consider this human proclivity, then we see that mankind is really in a sorry condition. Most everyone seems to be prejudiced against everybody else, including himself. Recently, a lady consulted me for severe anxiety with occasional attacks of panic and a generalized tendency toward irritability and tension. In exploring the problem, it was revealed that this lady had a preconceived idea about herself—that she was a super-competent person. This prejudice in favor of herself had become a liability in her life, since the frustrations and the experiences of daily living tended to challenge her preconceived notion about herself, and she lived in fear of having to realize that she was not really super-competent. What is social anxiety?

Comment: It is a fear of what people are thinking about us.

Comment: It is what you think about what others are thinking about what you are thinking.

Dr. Hora: It is also a fear of revealing what we are thinking about others.

Comment: We are afraid of being found out. We are afraid of someone finding out how unloving we are.

Dr. Hora: The Bible says, "Perfect love casteth out fear" (I John 4:18). In the context of what we were talking about until now, what would perfect love mean?

Comment: Having no preconceptions.

Comment: It is hard to be comfortable in a social situation until one has become loving. I went through a period when I could not speak in the company of others because of fear. Often I was sorry for having said something. Later, when I learned the meaning of being a beneficial presence, my fear left me and I could speak freely.

Dr. Hora: Isn't it interesting that we start out criticizing other people in order to make ourselves feel better. And the more we do this, the worse we are going to feel, because if we criticize others, we begin to hate them and we have unloving thoughts about them. So while we are making ourselves feel superior to them, we are building up a whole storehouse of thoughts which we would not want anyone to find out. We are living with a burdensome load of thoughts which we don't want anyone to know. Consequently, the more we try to feel better, the worse we feel. This way one cripples oneself socially. It becomes more and more difficult to communicate with one's fellow men and participate in the social process.

Another great danger is entertaining malicious thoughts. What are malicious thoughts?

Comment: It is when one enjoys thinking about someone else's misfortune.

Dr. Hora: How does an individual become malicious? By practicing thinking unloving thoughts about others, finding fault with others, blaming them. Pretty soon one begins to enjoy other people's misfortune. This way one gets caught up in a quagmire of malice. What is so special about malice? Malice is probably the psychological basis of malignant diseases. It is, therefore, very important to cleanse ourselves of all malicious thoughts. Never, never allow ourselves to entertain malicious thoughts under any circumstances, no matter what the provocation.

Comment: Sometimes when we are engaged in malicious fantasies, we are enjoying it and we don't want to admit to ourselves that we are malicious.

Dr. Hora: Nothing can hurt us more than fantasies, and of all the fantasies which we could possibly entertain, nothing is more dangerous than malicious fantasies.

Question: How then do we keep alert?

Dr. Hora: Everything in the material world and the physical body is only a manifestation of thoughts. Malicious thoughts will manifest themselves as malignant physical appearances. Our preconceptions about others are never valid; it is impossible to have a valid preconception about anybody.

Comment: Jesus said, "Love your enemies" (Matthew 5:44; Luke 6:27).

Dr. Hora: Yes. Some people may think that this is foolish, but it is profound wisdom. A valid existential principle is expressed in this statement: "Love thy enemies, bless them that curse you, do good to them that hate you, and pray for them which despitefully use you, and persecute you" (Matthew 5:44). What is cursing?

Comment: Cursing is malice.

Dr. Hora: Right. "Bless them that curse you." Nobody can hurt us as much as we ourselves with our own thoughts. Jesus also said, "A man's foes shall be they of his own household" (Matthew 10:36). What did he mean? Our own thoughts can be our undoing. Our greatest enemy is our own thought. St. Paul said, "Awake thou that sleepest, and arise from the dead, and Christ shall give thee light" (Ephesians 5:14). What does this mean?

Comment: When I am involved with fantasies, I don't want to wake up, I want to see them through.

Dr. Hora: What is the difference between thoughts, fantasies, and worries?

Comment: Thoughts are like birds flying over our heads, and fantasies are birds which nest in our hair.

Dr. Hora: Fantasies are pictorial thoughts; most of the time they involve imagination. There is calculative thinking; then there are fantasies which tend to be pleasurable; and then there is worry. Worry is also a form of fantasizing. It is fantasizing about what should not happen. So fantasy is making images about what should be, and worry is making images in the mind about what should not be.

Comment: And anxiety is that the fantasy wouldn't happen.

Dr. Hora: Or that we will be found out and be embarrassed. All these things are harmful and they are getting us nowhere. It would be desirable not to fantasize ever, not to worry ever, and not to think ever. Is that possible?

Comment: We are told that this is possible.

Dr. Hora: The famous French sculptor, Rodin, created a statue called *The Thinker*. This fellow is a miserable character, completely twisted around, with his left elbow resting on his right knee, and his face expressing despair. That's a thinker! Now beside this statue let us put the statue of the Buddha, sitting cross-legged with his hands folded and with a beautiful, peaceful, serene expression on his face. The first one is thinking, and what is this one doing? Is he thinking?

Comment: No.

Dr. Hora: He is not thinking? How is that possible? Is it possible in this world of ours to survive without thinking? Would Buddha survive in this world of ours?

Comment: But Dr. Hora, you didn't say what Buddha was doing. If he is not thinking, then what?

Dr. Hora: What is Buddha doing when he is sitting cross-legged, with his hands folded and serenely smiling, what is he doing?

Comment: Meditating.

Dr. Hora: Is it possible to live that way? Does it make any sense? Is it practical?

Comment: I hear that it is.

Dr. Hora: It is interesting to consider on the one hand this wretched character, the Thinker, who epitomizes everything our culture stands for—despair; and on the other hand to consider serene joy as expressed by the Buddha. One is thinking, the other is not thinking. How can we understand that? How is it possible? How can one live without thinking? Buddha is portrayed as sitting on a lotus blossom. What does that mean?

Comment: He is not very heavy.

Dr. Hora: He is not "a heavy." Thinkers are heavy, he is weightless.

Comment: He is not burdened.

Dr. Hora: He is not burdened and he is not a burden to anybody; he is only expressing serene joy. Ignorant people might be inclined to call him an idiot.

Comment: I was thinking that he is someone you wouldn't want to invite to a party.

Comment: Didn't Buddha say that he was awake? That reminds me of the quotation from the Bible about having to wake up.

Comment: It's hard for me to see how the Buddha could go through the day or make decisions.

Dr. Hora: A Buddha never makes decisions. Is that possible?

Comment: It is possible.

Dr. Hora: Now what is the difference between the Thinker

and the Buddha? Would you invite the Thinker to a party? He would kill your party with his despair.

Comment: I see Buddha as having total faith.

Dr. Hora: Buddha has no need for faith; he understands. Let us try to understand the difference between the Thinker and the Buddha.

Comment: The Thinker is there to entertain himself; he is living in his own fantasy. With the Buddha there is no fantasy involved.

Dr. Hora: Is that all?

Comment: The Thinker thinks he is the author of his own being.

Comment: I can see the Buddha expressing reverence and love, and the Thinker just doesn't know that.

Comment: The Buddha is immensely appreciative.

Dr. Hora: What do you mean by appreciative?

Comment: Of life and of beauty.

Dr. Hora: You really mean then that the Buddha is aware of certain values. Is that what you mean?

Comment: Yes.

Dr. Hora: That's a very good point. The Thinker is aware of his thoughts. What is the Buddha aware of?

Comment: The goodness of God.

Dr. Hora: What is that? The Buddha is aware of what is real. What is real?

Comment: Spiritual qualities.

Dr. Hora: Beauty is real, harmony is real, joy is real, peace is real, love is real, assurance is real, wisdom is real, freedom is real, perfect health is real, truth is real. These values are not thoughts, they are realities. The Thinker may try to think about these, but he does not know them; he may just know *about* them. But the Buddha is aware of them, and what we are aware of, we become. We are what we know. The Thinker does not know anything, he only knows about things.

Comment: He may even have faith.

Dr. Hora: Yes, but he is nowhere and he is nothing. He does not even exist he is fantasy. But the Buddha knows reality; therefore, he is real. What we know, that's what we are. What we think, that's what we seem to be. The Thinker is totally humorless, except perhaps in cruel ways. He can poke fun at the misfortune of other people. There is such a thing as "sick humor." When a Thinker makes a joke, he will always make it at the expense of someone else. However, there is also healthy humor. What is healthy humor based on?

Comment: Seeing things from a light point of view.

Comment: Laughing at absurdities, paradoxes of experience.

Dr. Hora: Yes. That is very funny and it is not at the expense of someone else. There is no cruelty in it, there is love and compassion and intelligence.

Suppose we are burdened with preconceived ideas about ourselves and others; we are tormented by worries and fascinated by fantasies. We are thinkers. What do we need? We need to be willing to be liberated from this human affliction, don't we? Who can save us? St. Paul says, "O wretched man that I am! Who shall deliver me from the body of this death?" (Romans 7:24). At one point he cried out in despair over himself because he was a Thinker, and it was hard for him to be liberated from a lifelong habit of intellectualism. We all need to be liberated from the thinking processes which obstruct our awareness and interfere with knowledge. Who will save us from the body of this death? How can we be liberated from being Thinkers?

We can be liberated through a process of prayer and meditation. We must practice being aware of spiritual values and learn to cherish or appreciate them—not thoughts *about* them but the values themselves—so that we might be transformed by what we know. Not what we know *about* but what we *know.* We must know beauty, we must know harmony, we must come to know love, truth, joy, freedom—these are realities. Recently I saw a short film clip about Arthur Rubinstein in which he was explaining what music means to him. He is now 90 years old and in good health, an extraordinary musician. He was explaining that to him music really means heavenly beauty. And he is aware of beauty as a reality of soul. To him beauty and harmony are not concepts. To most of us these are thoughts. We know about beauty, but to him beauty and harmony are actual realities. And these realities transformed him into being a beautiful harmonious individual. It keeps him alive and healthy.

In the proportion that we come to know these spiritual values as actual realities rather than thoughts about reality, in that proportion we become what we know. And if we are real, then we are immortal and perfect and everything is all right. So by practicing the awareness of these spiritual values we become liberated from the despair of being thinkers.

Dialogue No. 6

I AM THE LIGHT

Dr. Hora: We were asked to consider the problem of decision-making. We are all confronted with this problem every day. In general, there are two ways we tend to make decisions: one is a rational way and the other is an irrational way. What is the rational way?

Comment: To consider the pros and cons.

Dr. Hora: Right. Calculating the odds and options and adding up the score. Then there is the irrational way of making decisions, which is what?

Comment: I like it, so I will do it.

Dr. Hora: Right. It feels good, or I have a hunch, or somebody else said so, or flip a coin. There are many irrational techniques commonly used to make decisions. Well, which one is better, which one will you choose?

Comment: Neither one.

Dr. Hora: When it comes to decision-making, to be rational or to be irrational is the same. How is it possible? Isn't it smart to be rational?

Comment: Neither of these ways take into consideration the will of God.

Dr. Hora: There is another irrational way of decision-making and that's gambling, which is relying on chance. That, of course, is also a very poor way of making decisions.

Question: Isn't it also irrational to say, "I have prayed about it and I hope that it will turn out right"?

Dr. Hora: That is gambling on God. That is the religious approach.

Question: Would it be best to let go of the situation and not pray specifically for a decision but rather for peace and assurance and love, and to know that within that consciousness all things work together for good?

Dr. Hora: What do we call that kind of decision-making? This is the intelligent way. What makes it intelligent?

Comment: Relying on God.

Dr. Hora: Of course. The intelligent approach is based on the knowledge that it is presumptuous for man to think he can make decisions. If man were capable of making decisions, he would have to have a mind of his own, and that's absurd, isn't it? The intelligent way is to allow Love-Intelligence to show us the best way.

Comment: Sometimes, when we are willing to do that, some alternative will clearly define itself as preferable.

Question: How can one explain this process of right action on the basis of inspired wisdom without sounding knowledgeable?

Dr. Hora: We don't speak of what we know, we only speak of what comes. Is that clear?

Comment: In other words, instead of showing off with knowledge, we wait to see what is coming and then we say something.

Dr. Hora: That's right.

Comment: We can be aware of the presence of fresh ideas. And when we are aware that we are speaking on the basis of inspiration, we can go ahead. Then it is going to be helpful and good.

Dr. Hora: Motivation is fundamental. If our motivation is to shed light, to bless, to help, and to understand, then we are transparent, then the channel is open for Divine Intelligence to come through. But if the motivation is something else, then we are closed, turned off, and we are talking from our filing cabinet. You might say we can be a transparency or we can be a filing cabinet.

Comment: If you use your mind to impress people with how much you know, then you are a filing cabinet.

Dr. Hora: It is interesting that when we use words of the same language our sentences can be either dead or vibrant, with every word having the dynamism of life in it. The Bible says: "Who is this that darkeneth counsel by words without knowledge?" (Job 38:2). Sometimes we are shedding darkness. "If therefore the light that is in thee be darkness, how great is that darkness!" (Matthew 6:23).

Comment: That's awful!

Dr. Hora: We have to understand the difference between light and darkness, between being a transparency and being a filing cabinet. It is not at all difficult, it is very simple. It is nothing we have to do, it is just something we need to be aware of. It is not difficult to be enlightened, it is only difficult to be interested in enlightenment.

Comment: I am more interested in confirming myself and I am not aware that this is illegitimate.

Dr. Hora: Bragging is not illegitimate, it is just troublesome. We do not say you should not brag, we say it is troublesome to brag. We never speak about what should be or what shouldn't be. We only speak about what seems to be and point at what really is. It makes life very simple.

Question: Is it what we say or how we say it that matters? Is it the words or the motivation behind the words?

Dr. Hora: It is everything.

Comment: When we are asked a question, it is important to unmask the hidden question behind the question.

Dr. Hora: Yes. Can you unmask the question which was just asked—whether it is the words that matter or how the question is asked?

Comment: It is an operational question.

Dr. Hora: Yes. Its meaning is: How could I talk in such a way as to make it appear like a real question? What is this great urge to get away with things? It is the instinct of self-preservation. We are most reluctant to die, but nothing else will do. The ego must die. The futile questions nourish the ego and keep it alive. So we are most reluctant to refrain from asking the futile questions, and we are twisting and turning, trying to find a roundabout way of asking them anyway.

If we want to be resurrected to spiritual life, we must be willing to let the ego die. "He that findeth his life shall lose it: and he that loseth his life for my sake shall find it" (Matthew 10:39). When we refrain from "should" thinking and "want" thinking and from asking the futile questions, we are allowing the ego to die. What did Job do just before he became enlightened? He put his hand over his mouth and shut up. And then he saw the light. "I have heard of thee by the hearing of the ear; but now mine eye seeth thee" (Job 42:5). He came to see what really is.

Of course, silence alone will not do it. In certain monasteries there are periods of silence. The monks or nuns go through days or weeks when they are not allowed to say a word. Does that help? Of course not. The "shouldn't" becomes a punishment, and the "should" will never help us to become "shouldless." Only understanding can help us to become shouldless. And understanding does not come in silence, and it does not come in talking. How does it come? In right talking, in talking the right way.

In the group situation we can make our mistakes with relative impunity, and we have the advantage of being shown what the mistake is. So it is a comfortable situation, structured for increasing the awareness of our mistakes so that we may be spared the consequences of these mistakes in daily life. If we are protecting ourselves from embarrassment through isolation, then going out into a group situation may make it much worse. So there is no advantage to sitting back and protecting oneself from embarrassment. Jesus covered this contingency too. As quoted before: "Whosoever will save his life [face] shall lose it" (Matthew 16:25). Of course, one can protect oneself either by talking or by not talking. The carnal mind is as devious and flexible as a snake, but nothing is gained by protecting oneself, for we are only protecting the ego and the ego must go sooner or later.

"I want" is self-righteous; "I should" is willful; "I like" is self-indulgent. The important thing is not to think in terms of healing but in terms of perfect life. As long as we are focusing on healing, we will have a vested interest in sickness because without sickness there is no healing. And beware of what you set your heart on. We are not really interested in healing, we are interested in knowing and seeing that everything everywhere is already all right. No imperfection can enter true being. If we are interested in teaching, we have a vested interest in perpetuating ignorance.

MEDITATION

Question: Is Transcendental Meditation something beneficial?

Dr. Hora: Before we can ask whether something is beneficial, it would be better to ask, what is it? What do you think TM is?

Comment: I attended some lectures on it and, if I understand it correctly, it is supposed to be a technique which gives the body a fourth dimension of rest which is better than sleep. It seems to me that there is too much emphasis on what it does to the body. I am not sure, however, whether I understand what it really is.

Comment: Someone said that it is like taking a sauna bath.

Dr. Hora: TM is all right. It cannot hurt. It has great value for relaxation, but you must understand that it is neither meditation nor is it transcendental.

Comment: I don't understand that.

Dr. Hora: Meditation is a form of prayer, and this seems to be more a form of concentration on a mantra. However, there is value in considering this technique. It shows us clearly that the body is not responsible for anything; that if we have a pain, the pain is not really in the body. If we have a physical illness, the illness is not really in the body, it is in the thoughts which we harbor in consciousness. And if we are tired, it is not the body that is tired, but rather the disturbing ideas which we then interpret as tiredness. Now comes the Maharishi who says: "Close your eyes and repeat your secret word . . ." and you disengage your attention from disturbing thoughts. And you will experience favorable physiological effects. The body gets a rest because the thought processes are being shunted aside and temporarily silenced. The blood pressure responds, the heartbeat slows down, the muscles relax, the aches and pains disappear temporarily. But it is just a way of inducing peace and, so to speak, "quieting the monkey," the restless monkey.

Comment: Agitated thoughts.

Dr. Hora: Right. The personal mind. And what does this personal mind think about? What is it agitated about? First of all, this personal mind is thinking about what others are thinking about what it is thinking; this is the most frequent occurrence. Further, this personal mind is thinking about why somebody is the way he is, and who is to blame for the way he is, what he should do that he should not be the way he is, and how he should do it. For the most part, this is what is going on in the personal mind, and we are not aware of it except as we become more sophisticated. Otherwise, all that we are aware of are physical sensations, aches and pains, pressures and headaches, jitteriness and restlessness. So, in a sense, TM is a simple method which anyone can learn and use with some benefit. But, of course, if we stop there, this restless monkey resumes its activity. Real transcendence means to go beyond the personal mind, to become aware of a mind which is larger than the personal mind—the divine Mind.

Comment: I would like to report a situation that, I suppose, came about by relying on something beyond the personal mind. For a long time I used to get very tired; I could sleep half the day away although I wasn't really involved in doing anything very exhausting. I have always believed that a certain number of hours of sleep was required in order to wake up with energy and some desire to continue on. Recently, I was working in a restaurant, and as the weeks progressed, the working hours became longer and longer. At first I was just exhausted, but I knew that if I could make contact with the source of energy, it would start flowing and I would not have to do anything or use up all my energies. I started to pray in this manner and tried to see myself as an emanation of God, that it was God's energy and strength that would be needed to perform this work. A quotation from the Bible kept coming to me: "But they that wait upon the Lord shall renew their strength; they shall mount up with wings as eagles; they shall run, and not be weary; and they shall walk and not faint" (Isaiah 40:31). I kept thinking about this during the day and the most amazing thing happened. It seemed I did not require sleep any more; I seemed able to work all the time. Yesterday I got up at 5:15 in the morning, baked 20 pies, and worked as a hostess at lunch time when we served 650 lunches. After lunch I continued to bake for the evening, and then did some bookkeeping. I came home late at night and was not really tired. It was just an extraordinary experience, and it was clearly the effect of my prayer which made it possible.

Comment: It is good to hear this because if there is one thing we all have in common, it is that we all have so much to do and the frustration of fatigue can be great.

Dr. Hora: It is only the restless monkey of the personal mind that gets tired. It is like a little child that is always jumping around and wearing himself out. Once we can see that there is really no such thing as a restless monkey, that it is an illusion, then everything that the monkey has ever produced is also an illusion, including tiredness and restlessness. Then we are in contact with infinite Mind, which has infinite power, and "He that keepeth Israel shall neither slumber nor sleep" (Psalm 121:4).

So, transcendental is that which transcends the human mind, the human condition, the human illusion. Now what is meditation? Under the term meditation a multitude of self-deceptions can be found. Some people say: I have taken up TM. I am meditating. But they may just be daydreaming. In TM, meditation consists of mumbling subvocally a certain Sanskrit word to oneself. This is called the mantra. Another method is based on chanting; that also has some value. Then there is twirling, like the dervishes do in Suffism. These are all endeavors to put the personal mind out of commission temporarily, but it is not really meditation. What is meditation?

Comment: Meditation is really reaching a point where we get a response in the form of an idea from the creative Mind; essentially it is listening.

Dr. Hora: If we want to consider the issue of meditation in greater detail, we have to clarify several phases of meditation. The first phase is prayer, which is verbal. We can talk to ourselves, perhaps making an affirmation such as, God is Love; reciting a Psalm or the Lord's Prayer; or reading a passage in the Bible. That is the verbal initial phase of meditation. We proceed step by step.

The second phase is nonverbal and this is called contemplation, where we are getting more and more quiet and are contemplating the nature of divine reality nonverbally, just in thought. Contemplation proceeds to the point of beholding. What is beholding?

Comment: Knowing.

Dr. Hora: Right. Reaching beyond thought. First, there are words, then there are thoughts, and then there is beholding. Then comes the third phase, which is beyond words and thoughts. It is absolute stillness, awareness, listening and hearing. Then there is PAGL. And when PAGL comes, we know that we have really been in meditation, we have journeyed into the Kingdom of God, into spiritual consciousness —and that's what meditation is.

To summarize, meditation consists of the following progression: verbal, nonverbal, contemplative, beholding, listening, hearing, and PAGL. This is transcendental and it is meditation. Now, as far as effects are concerned, what can be expected from real meditation?

Comment: Transformation of outlook on life and of our mode of being-in-the-world.

Dr. Hora: TM gives relaxation; real meditation heals, transforms the entire outlook on life, and even affects man's circumstances.

Dialogue No. 8

AFFLUENCE

Question: What is the secret of affluence?

Dr. Hora: Cheerful generosity. The principle is this: Affluence is in proportion to effluence. The more outflow, the more inflow.

Comment: We also have to know the source of our income. Is it our job or something else? Something interesting happened to me recently. I was invited to go on a cruise next spring. I have never been on a cruise, and I realized that I am not inclined to go on vacations and spend a lot of money. But I have been able to see many unusual places and I don't have to pay for them. There is a principle at work here which shows that it doesn't seem to matter whether or not I have the money. This is also a good lesson for me because I always think that money comes from my job. There is something else at work here; generosity is reflected in generosity.

Dr. Hora: What is money?

Comment: A medium of exchange.

Dr. Hora: Right. In commerce. But metaphysically it is the shadow of love. What do we mean by that? Love is something that is of vital importance to all of us, and it flows from an unlimited source. There will never be a time when we will run out of love. It is impossible to run dry as far as love is concerned. The right understanding of love and its free expression will reveal to us that money is the shadow of love. Love is spiritual substance, money is material shadow. The more love is allowed to flow freely, the more generous we become, and the shadow will always keep pace with the substance. Wherever we go our shadow goes with us, there is no way *we* can escape it. Where love flows freely in the form of generosity, affection, and good will, there is an abundance of money, and there is affluence.

Question: What about behaving in a loving way when we think we should be loving? Where do we start if we don't think we are generous?

Dr. Hora: The moment we think that we should be loving and kind, we have already blocked the source of love. If it is a "should," we are defeated before we start.

Question: Would it be better to say: I am generous, but I need to see more clearly that this is so?

Dr. Hora: That's a good point. So let us be careful about the "should" because where should enters into thought, the awareness of God is blocked out. Love is, generosity is, affluence is. We become aware of it. Someone might say that awareness is a "should," but it is not a "should"; it is grace. We cannot make it. If we could "should" the awareness, then we would become very self-righteous about it; we could say, "I did it."

Comment: I guess that's where sincere interest comes in. If we are sincerely interested in understanding this, then it is available to us.

Dr. Hora: By the grace of God we become aware and we come to understand the principle of affluence. If we are materialistically minded, if we think of money in material terms, then we will always be poor no matter how much money we earn. There are people who get tremendous salaries and the cannot make ends meet. We have to understand that money is not substance, money is the shadow of real substance. The material world is the shadow of reality. Reality is spiritual, everything real is spiritual.

Today a lovely young lady spoke about her fears of going out on a date because she thinks herself to be too fat and unattractive. So she was told not to think of herself as flesh. There are men who think of women as as "pieces of meat" and, even worse, as things. And there are women who have accepted this idea, and who think of themselves in material terms and worry about it. That is what materialism does, it makes people fearful, insecure, and troubled.

It is amazing how stingy we can be with our affections and good will, as if it might cost us money. Sometimes one hears people say: "Well, it doesn't cost you money to say hello, to be friendly, or to smile." Is it any wonder that there is the experience of financial lack?

Comment: Would you please define affection?

Dr. Hora: Affection is the human equivalent of divine love, the human manifestation of divine love.

Question: How about good will?

Dr. Hora: Good will, again, is the human expression of the will of God. God wants us to be beneficial presences in the world, and that includes emotional generosity.

Comment: Without pretense.

Dr. Hora: Without pretense, strictly on the basis of understand g the principle of perfect God and his perfect expression—man. The perfect manifestation of Love-Intelligence. Of course, there are people who are generous with counterfeit love, and these people may become very rich with counterfeit money that buys nothing.

Comment: I have seen this happen at home. There is a certain misunderstanding among people of my faith who give to charity so that they will be blessed.

Dr. Hora: This is an interesting idea to consider. According to biblical scholars, the Bible speaks of charity as a synonym for love. But charity, according to our understanding, means giving to the poor. Giving to the poor is, most of the time, a nuisance; and the idea of charity has become completely divorced from the idea of love. Yet, existentially, charity and love belong together. We have to be very charitable with our love, which means being generous with it. Being charitable means being generous. So we don't say: We are charitable with our money, we give charity. But sometimes we can say: He is very charitable with his affection and good will; he is very kind, very generous, very thoughtful. It is important to redeem the word "charity" and to practice charitableness as a form of generosity with love. Whether we are giving material objects, money, assistance, or anything else, if we give it in the right spirit, then we are being charitable.

If we are giving charity in the spirit of our culture, we are just looking for a good tax deduction, or bribing people and

God. And this kind of charitableness has no existential value, neither on an individual scale nor on a national scale. We have been giving millions of dollars to poor nations with no real benefit to anyone. If we are being charitable in the wrong spirit, it usually backfires. But if we are charitable, that is, generous in the right spirit, what will happen? Affluence will result. We are then opening the floodgates of abundance of the divine good will on all levels, and the result is affluence. The more we give, the more we have to give; the more generous and charitable we are, the more affluent we become. This is the law of affluence. But it is a spiritual law, and human calculative thinking will never do. Charity for the sake of being blessed usually occurs when an unenlightened person is instructed in some religious "shoulds" without understanding the principle behind it, and he does what he "should" do. What happens in religion is that the existential principles stated by various spiritual seers become invaded by the crabgrass of "should" thinking. Thus we have religions that have become existentially irrelevant. People are giving to charity to earn themselves rewards and in the hope that God will take notice and perhaps smile at them with approval.

Question: Tithing is supposed to be giving ten percent of your income. Where does this come from?

Dr. Hora: The moment we set a certain standard, we introduce a "should." The moment we introduce an arbitrary figure, we have introduced a "should" thought, which is the basis of obsessive-compulsive religiosity. It pollutes the principle of divine reality. By becoming "shouldless" we move from religion to enlightenment.

Question: What is the meaning of the religious requirement of giving of the firstfruits?

Dr. Hora: It is giving we cherish most. Usually, we cherish the firstfruits most. The purpose of this is to discipline ourselves not to cherish anything except the love of being loving and the love of being generous But again, we must guard against "should" thinking. Someone said, it is written in the Bible what we should do and how we should do it, and the moment we accept the "should" thought, we have closed the door to understanding and we have become religious. Religion interferes with the knowledge of God. That does not mean that we must reject religion, but we must be alerted to the necessity of going beyond conventional religion.

When we are being generous we are not doing a favor to anybody, we are bringing ourselves into alignment with a great power, the power of divine abundance.

Comment: When I am here, my understanding of God is much better and purer, but when I am in other situations, when I am resentful, God has no reality to me and I don't understand him.

Dr. Hora: Perhaps it would be helpful here to have a clearer understanding of what prayer is. Is prayer a "How?" or is prayer a "What?" If we understand prayer as a searching for what really is, then we would not have to ask, "How do I get from here to there?" "How do I get out of the garbage into the kingdom of God?" We do not have to get out of the garbage; the garbage is not real and the kingdom of God is. So we do not have to ask, "How?" but "What?" Whenever we ask "How?" we are committing two errors: one is giving reality to what is not real; the second is giving reality to the belief that we can do something on our own power.

Comment: First we learn that operating doesn't do any good. Then we learn that not operating is operating, and that also doesn't do any good.

Comment: I have a hard time turning things over to God and letting him be in control. How does one let God make decisions?

Dr. Hora: What is the meaning of "How?"

Comment: A false sense of responsibility.

Dr. Hora: The meaning of "How?" points toward operationalism. The "How?" must be replaced by a "What?" and then there will be no problem. This may sound very mysterious but it is really simple. If we understand the difference between "How?" and "What?" everything will become clear.

Comment: "How?" refers to our own power.

Dr. Hora: Right. The moment we ask the right question, at that moment we are entering divine reality where there are no problems, no fears, where everyone is intelligent and does the right thing at the right time in the right way, effortlessly and always. Nothing bad happens in divine reality. But as long as we ask "How?" we are not interested in living in divine reality, we are interested in human ingenuity and power. Therefore, the "How?" is a stumbling block which prevents us from entering into divine reality. Only the "What?" can open the door to divine reality. The moment we enter divine reality, there is peace, assurance, gratitude, and love. No more agonizing over decisions and choices and what should be and what should not be.

Comment: I used to be so caught up in the desire to be in charge of everything that the only thing I could see was the "How?" and I could not in any way be humble. It seems that what was needed was to ask: "What must I know?" It was impossible for me to ask "What?" I didn't realize it until just now that I had to be in charge of everything always.

Dr. Hora: When we are sincerely asking "What is what really *is?*" then PAGL will descend on us like a white dove. This question is the knocking on the door of reality and "to him that knocketh, it shall be opened" (Matthew 7:8; Luke 11:10).

Dialogue No. 9

WHO IS IN CONTROL?

Question: I have a question about unseeing appearances. I have never really been able to "unsee" something that appears to be evil, and I wonder what the problem is. For instance, I took the dogs out for a walk and I was trying to see them as God's harmonious creatures. But they acted like idiots, as they always do. I would like to see them walking nicely, but it never happens.

Comment: You are thinking about how the dogs *should* act.

Dr. Hora: You speak about unseeing, but what do you really mean? You reveal that you have a certain idea about unseeing. What do you mean?

Comment: You want to use spirital ideas to control the behavior of your dogs. You are thinking of using God to remedy the situation.

Dr. Hora: It is wrong to control people and animals humanly, and it is wrong to control them spiritually. What are we here for? Are we here to learn the secret technique of exercising effective control over people and animals, over friends and foes? What are we here for?

Comment: To come to appreciate and recognize God's control.

Dr. Hora: That's right.

Comment: It often happens that I start out the day with the thought of doing the will of God, but something happens and pretty soon things are getting chaotic; by midafternoon I am just drifting in confusion. It seems that circumstances are controlling me.

Dr. Hora: What are you really describing? You are saying, "Things are out of control." The dogs are out of control, the children are out of control, and the household is out of control. What is the meaning of things being out of control?

Comment: It must mean that they are trying to be in control of their affairs.

Dr. Hora: What are we learning here?

Comment: That God is in control.

Dr. Hora: What does that mean?

Comment: We receive intelligent ideas from God and these, in turn, help us to do our daily chores efficiently and harmoniously and well.

Dr. Hora: What do we mean when we say that Love-Intelligence, the harmonizing principle of the universe, governs all? What does God control? Does God control the dogs for us? What does God control? God controls our thoughts, if we let him. How do we let him? How do we become God-centered in our thinking? We are all professing interest in God-centered thinking.

Suppose we are sitting in a movie theater together and there is a bad but fascinating picture on the screen. As we get involved with this picture, we begin to get sick. Now what is happening? The movie has sucked us in and is gaining control over us. It is called "enjoying" and experiencing a film. But suppose that we are alert enough to know that we are in trouble, that we have been taken over by this movie and it is hurting us. How do we now control this movie so that it shouldn't do to us what it is doing to us?

Comment: I think what is needed is to understand that we are taken in by an illusion, and to understand what really is.

Dr. Hora: How do you do that? Just saying that this is illusion or garbage and that it is not good does nothing. As a matter of fact, things may get worse because we may get more and more involved with the movie in a negative way. Because yes is no, and no is double yes.

Question: Suppose I close my eyes?

Dr. Hora: You will still have the thoughts of the movie in your consciousness, and you will still be in the power of the movie.

Comment: You have to devote your attention somehow to something better.

Dr. Hora: Your neighbor, perhaps?

Comment: We have to become aware of God through prayer and meditation.

Dr. Hora: Yes, we endeavor to disengage our attention from the movie by turning to God, and we seek to be aware of the presence of God to such an extent that we completely lose sight of the movie and become aware that Love-Intelligence is right there with us. And as we sincerely and gratefully contemplate the presence of Love-Intelligence, we begin to be under control of God instead of the movie. And what happens when God takes control of our being, of our consciousness? All those things will disappear, the movie fades out of our awareness and we are filled with a sense of peace and assurance, of gratitude and love. We are safe and God is in control of our lives.

The more we learn to turn wholeheartedly to the awareness of Love-Intelligence as an omnipresent reality, the more this Love-Intelligence takes control not only of our consciousness but of our environment. Everything comes under the control of this infinite power and love and intelligence, and things begin to work together for good.

When we speak of movies, we use it of course as an illustration of all life situations. Because all horizontal transactions in the world are nothing but movies, and all discord and strife and misery are all movies, and we do not have to enjoy these movies, we can disengage our attention and refocus it on God, Love-Intelligence, and let it take over our affairs. God helps those who *let* him.

Comment: Something happened to me today which illustrated this principle very clearly. This afternoon I discovered that my wallet was missing. I couldn't for the life of me figure out what had happened to it. I wondered what I should do, and what would I do now? It was as if my identity had disappeared, and I started to think that perhaps I should blame someone. After a while, the idea came to me that God helps those who let him, and all of a sudden it occurred to me that there was one place during the day where I still had my wallet and I went back there. It was on a floor below me in an industrial building that was being demolished. I went to this place where there was a pile of rubbish and a cardboard box. I looked into the box and my wallet was in there.

Dr. Hora: This is a good illustration of the principle we were talking about, how divine intelligence takes over and controls our impulses.

Comment: It absolutely proved it to me.

Dr. Hora: What you did so successfully was to disengage your attention from the futile questions, which most people ask in such situations, and turn your attention to a principle: God helps those who let him. Not only did you declare this principle, but you actually allowed it to take over control of you and you obeyed the impulse to look in the right place which was inspired by divine intelligence.

Question: Would it have interfered had he said, "God helps those who let him and he will find the wallet"? Is that already outlining what should be?

Dr. Hora: Yes. It is already contaminating the principle with a "should." There is something more important than the wallet. What is more important? The principle is more important than the wallet.

What is prayer and meditation?

Comment: Spiritual thinking.

Dr. Hora: What is spiritual thinking? Spiritual thinking is thinking about spiritual issues. Is there such a thing as thinking? Material thinking or spiritual thinking? Let us go back to the movies. When the pictures are moving on the screen, what is happening in our consciousness? Thinking is taking place. We have the illusion that we are thinking the thoughts the picture is suggesting; but we are not really thinking those thoughts, we are allowing certain thoughts to pass through our awareness. Our consciousness is an empty screen and it is either filled with garbage—and then we have the illusion that we are thinking—or we disengage our attention from the garbage and refocus our interest on God. And what happens then? The garbage disappears, as far as we are concerned, and intelligent ideas begin gently to engage our attention.

It is therefore important to know that we cannot think at all. But we can choose to be interested either in garbage or in

Love-Intelligence. So when in prayer and meditation we shift our attention to God, infinite Mind, and allow our awareness to dwell on it, we begin to receive intelligent ideas appropriate to our need of the moment. So God becomes our mind and takes over our lives and, as we allow it, things begin to be accomplished harmoniously, effortlessly, and perfectly. So how do we define prayer and meditation on the basis of what we have just said? It is not telling God what he should do. What is prayer and meditation? Prayer and meditation is letting Love-Intelligence take over our affairs and fill us with energy, vitality, intelligent ideas, inspired wisdom, joy, love, assurance. Whence cometh assurance? There are millions of people who suffer a great deal of anxiety from a lack of a sense of assurance. Whence cometh it? The more often we practice becoming aware of the presence of Love-Intelligence as a sustaining reality of our life, of our being, the more assurance we gain, and we may not even know what anxiety is, or ever was. It will just disappear as the movie disappears when we disengage our attention from it.

Comment: You cannot show movies where there is light.

Dr. Hora: Sometimes the movies are not on a screen but in imagination. Can we disengage our attention from internal movies equally as well as those projected onto a screen?

Comment: I am sure it is the same.

Dr. Hora: Suppose someone has a headache. He is not in the movies but at home. Does the same principle apply? Certainly, but usually we are reluctant to know the title of the movie which is playing inside because it is too embarrassing. It helps if we are willing to be embarrassed. Usually it is embarrassing to realize that we are so foolish as to allow ourselves to be fascinated by a silly movie, but it helps us to disengage our attention from the internal movie and turn wholeheartedly to the task of becoming aware that God is our life, and God is our good, and God is the power which can most effectively handle our affairs if we let him. But we must be so appreciative of God that we can really disengage our attention from the movie and not be mesmerized by it.

Dialogue No. 10

WHAT IS GOOD?

Question: I have an itch of long standing. It does not itch me at work but mostly when I am at home. I would like to know why it is so.

Dr. Hora: When we ask the question "Why?" we don't get anywhere.

Comment: I think the meaning of it is ambitious thinking, competitive thinking. But what I don't understand is why in the working environment, where there is more competition, it is less troublesome than at home. I would like to know the reason for this.

Dr. Hora: Reason is also a "Why?" Cause, reason, and "Why?" are the same. If we want to have an answer, we must ask the right question.

Comment: There seems to be two questions here. First, what is the meaning of the itch? Second, is it gratified during the day?

Dr. Hora: Perhaps the question is this: What is the meaning of an itching itch, and what is the meaning of a non-itching itch? Is that the question you wanted to ask?

Comment: Yes.

Question: How is a non-itching itch an itch?

Dr. Hora: A non-itching itch is an itch which is temporarily dormant. Where is your itch?

Comment: In my toes.

Dr. Hora: That's interesting. You could say that those are itchy toes.

Comment: I think he has ambition in his toes.

Comment: Maybe he has ambition to get ahead, or to kick somebody.

Dr. Hora: Be that as it may, it is safe to assume that an itch is always a desire. The desire may be varied. Sometimes we desire our desires more desirously than at other times. When does our desire become more active?

Comment: When we are frustrated.

Dr. Hora: There is another important factor, too. When we are in the presence of someone who has a similar desire, then these two desires potentiate themselves. Some people encourage one another in certain directions overtly, covertly, or subliminally. What desires are most common?

Comment: Power.

Dr. Hora: Yes. Could be.

Comment: Sensual desires.

Dr. Hora: Sensual desire, a desire for sensory pleasure. That is one of the most frequent desires. The most primitive idea of what is good is the idea of sensory pleasure. The infant's first acquaintance with pleasure is sensory; later on he discovers emotional gratification; still later on, intellectual excitement. We can say that the most elementary of all desires is the desire for sensory pleasure. This is universal. If we ask anyone what he wants most in life, he will most likely say sex and good food. It is really of very little importance whether the itch is at home or on the job, knowing the difference would not facilitate the healing of it. If anyone wants to be healed of itching, he needs to be healed of sensualism. What is sensualism?

Comment: It is a belief that the good is sensory.

Dr. Hora: That's right. As we said, the most common and primitive belief is that the good of life is sensory or emotional or intellectual. But is it? What is the good of life? Someone might say, the good of life is money. How would we classify this?

Comment: Materialism.

Dr. Hora: I know a lady who is not interested in sensualism or emotionalism or intellectualism; only in antique furniture.

Comment: When we say that sensualism is a belief that the good of life is sensory, what is the relationship of that idea to the idea that sensualism is a desire to confirm oneself through the senses? How do these seemingly different statements relate to each other?

Dr. Hora: There are five ways we can engage in self-confirmatory activity. These are the five gates of hell: sensualism, materialism, emotionalism, intellectualism, and personalism. Unenlightened life consists of five different ways of saying the same thing: "I am." Enlightened man, of course, discovers that this is a mistake, and he does not have the desire to say "I am" anymore. What does he want to say?

Comment: He wants to say, "God is."

Dr. Hora: That's right. A radical shift has taken place in his outlook on life and what constitutes the good, the *summum bonum vitae*. What does that mean?

Comment: The supreme good of life.

Dr. Hora: When we are oriented toward saying that, then all the itches and scratches, the bellyaches and headaches, all these things disappear, vanish. And what do we have? We have the good of God. What is the good of God?

Comment: The good of God is peace, assurance, gratitude, love, beauty, harmony, freedom, joy, and so on.

Comment: Clarity. Just to be able to see and not be confused.

Dr. Hora: Can we say, I am itching to know the good of God?

Comment: No.

Dr. Hora: What can we say?

Comment: I am dying to know the good of God.

Comment: That's not bad.

Dr. Hora: The good of God is difficult to know.

Comment: I never heard you say that. You usually say that everything is easy.

Dr. Hora: What makes the good of God difficult to know?

Comment: Lack of interest.

Dr. Hora: It is inconceivable.

Comment: Unthinkable.

Dr. Hora: It is unthinkable, unimaginable, invisible, and intangible.

Comment: But real.

Dr. Hora: Isn't it interesting? Doesn't that turn our entire world upside down? Or right side up?

Comment: That was such a wonderful summary. We have

listed all the things that make it difficult to see; then the fact that it is real, clinches the whole thing. It was almost liturgical.

Comment: This makes it clear that to confer any kind of reality on unreality is absurd.

Comment: I noticed that people don't know that they don't know.

Dr. Hora: What practical value is there in knowing the good of God?

Comment: There is incredible value in knowing the good of God, but not in knowing about the good of God.

Dr. Hora: Jesus said, "Take no thought for the body, nor for your life in the body, nor for what you will drink, nor for what you will wear. For after all these things do the Gentiles seek." What did he mean by that?

Comment: The unenlightened.

Dr. Hora: That's right. Unenlightened man is forever thinking about feelings and sensations, his life in the body, his clothes, his food, his drink, his emotions, his possessions. That's what life seems to be. But Jesus said don't think about those things. "Seek ye first the kingdom of God, and his righteousness; and all these things shall be added unto you" (Matthew 6:33). What is the kingdom of God?

Comment: It is the good of God.

Dr. Hora: Yes. Jesus says to pay attention and seek to become aware of the good of God and all these things shall be added unto you. It would be very helpful under all circumstances to learn the art of beholding the good of God, which is synonymous with seeking the kingdom of God.

Question: Is beholding the good the same as gratitude?

Dr. Hora: No, gratitude is acknowledging the good of God, and that can be intellectual or emotional. Beholding the good is seeing it with our inward eye. Has anyone ever seen with his inward eye? What is the inward eye? The Hindus call it *Dhyana* or *Prajna-Paramita;* the Buddhists speak of *Darma.*

Comment: The Bible speaks of the single eye.

Dr. Hora: Yes, that has something to do with it. "If thine eye be single, thy whole body shall be full of light" (Matthew 6:22). In other words, if we can behold the good of God with the inward eye, we can be healed. It is possible to learn, through the practice of prayer and meditation, to develop the capacity of beholding. And right where problems seem to be, we can behold the good of God, especially if we understand that problems belong in that world of illusion which consists of the five gates of hell. Problems can only be sensual, emotional, intellectual, material, or personal.

If we are confronted with a problem that is staring us in the eye, we can say: I am not going to get involved with this. I will be seeking to behold the good of God right where this problem seems to be. Whenever we are able to lose sight of what seems to be and to know what really is, we can invariably expect a healing to occur. Isn't it fantastic? The moment we turn our attention to beholding the good of God, we are at one with the good. We are the good, and the good is. "I am in the Father, and the Father in me" (John 14:11). "I and my Father are one" (John 10:30). There is no place for a problem to be.

Comment: I have a great need to understand more about prayer. We were told that problems thrive on attention, and if we could only refuse to nourish the problem by withdrawing our attention from it even for a split second, we could then pray effectively. Now the question is: How do we loosen the grip that the problem has on us?

Dr. Hora: Can anyone suggest a way of moving from the problem to its solution?

Comment: The problem does not have a grip on us; we have a grip on the problem.

Dr. Hora: That's right. What is the meaning of not letting go of the problem? It would be helpful and practically relevant to understand the meaning of the difficulty of letting go of a problem. What could be the meaning of that?

Comment: In Alcoholics Anonymous they have a slogan: "Let go and let God." But if God is not in the picture at all, if we do not think that God is present, we will not even consider letting go of the problem.

Dr. Hora: You just described one of the possible factors in this phenomenon, the meaning of which is that we want to solve our own problems. As long as we have difficulty in letting go of our problems, it means that we are trying to solve them for ourselves and by ourselves. It is like trying to lift ourselves by our bootstraps. So what is the remedy for this nonreflective impulse to handle our own problems?

Comment: It means that we believe that we have the power to control our own lives.

Dr. Hora: Well, aren't we intelligent people, able to solve our own problems?

Comment: Sometimes I think we are only like puppets of God, and I find this idea very disturbing.

Comment: That would imply a separation between God and man.

Question: Then what is a better way of seeing it?

Comment: Sometimes we say: All right, I can see that I can not do it, so I am going to pray to God and let him do it. Then we would be trying to tell God what he should do, and that is not letting go of the problem either. The answer to problem-solving is not for God to solve the problem; God does not solve the problem.

Dr. Hora: Right.

Comment: I would think that the key issue would be beholding what really is.

Dr. Hora: That's a very good point. We are not problem-solvers; neither is God, nor a psychiatrist—nor are we puppets. We are not even healers. The Bible says, "I am the Lord that healeth thee" (Exodus 15:26). Also, "Bless the Lord, O my soul . . . who healeth all thy diseases" (Psalm 103:1, 3). How does God do it?

Comment: If we behold what really is, this dissolves what seems to be and the problem is gone.

Dr. Hora: When there is a problem, the first thing to do is not to try to solve it. Suppose we are sick; the first impulse is to try to cure ourselves of the sickness, take something, eat something, not eat something. But we are forced to realize that there is nothing we can do. The second point to realize is that neither can God do anything, so it is no use praying to him about the problem. It is no use going to the psychiatrist so that he should do something. What is there left?

Comment: A sense of helplessness and despair.

Dr. Hora: We can either try to see something by ourselves or with the help of someone who is able to see, and that helps. We are not problem-solvers, neither are we healers; but we are would-be seers. We have to see something. If there is a problem, the first thing is to see something, and the more clearly we can see something that is real, the more quickly will the problem be solved or the healing will come. This seeing is called "beholding." What kind of seeing is beholding? It is not ordinary seeing. What are we using in this kind of seeing?

Comment: We do not use anything, we see with our being.

Dr. Hora: This is rather difficult to understand, isn't it?

Comment: You said it is inconceivable.

Dr. Hora: It is inconceivable and yet we must learn to see this way. Has anyone ever seen love? I will tell you a secret. Many people might say that they felt love, but love is not a feeling. Many people will say: "Oh, I know what love is, it is a word, l-o-v-e." Or they will say it is a concept, a thought, a way of thinking about somebody. None of these things is love. Love is not a word, it is not a thought, and it is not a feeling or sensation. Love is not intellectual, emotional, sensual, material, or personal. What is it?

Comment: Love *is,* and when it is, we all see that it really is.

Dr. Hora: How do we see it? What does it look like?

Comment: It is like the wind. You don't see the wind, only its effects.

Dr. Hora: That is what Jesus meant when he said: "The wind bloweth where it listeth, and thou hearest the sound thereof, but canst not tell whence it cometh, and whither it goeth: so is everyone that is born of the Spirit" (John 3:8). In beholding we endeavor to be aware of love, of beauty, of goodness, of truth, of joy, of freedom, and of peace in their pure reality. We can be in existential contact with the pure reality, which is neither a thought, nor a feeling, nor a concept, nor anything else. That is how we can behold God, divine reality. That is the kind of seeing we need to learn if we want our problems to disappear.

Question: What is the process of meditation? How can we reach the point of beholding?

Comment: With the help of the two intelligent questions. By contemplating the question: "What is the meaning of what seems to be?" And: "What is what really *is?*"

Dr. Hora: We seek the meaning only to use it in juxtaposition with what really *is.* If we understand the meaning of a problem, then it is a little easier to behold what really *is* by contrast. For instance, if we would have said "Why is it that we cannot tear ourselves away from our problems? Why is it that we cannot let go of the problem?" there would be all sorts of explanations—the problem is too serious, too urgent, too difficult. And if we ask "Who is to blame for our problem?" then we are just trying to make ourselves feel better temporarily by blaming it on someone. And if we ask "What should I do about it?" then we are really getting deeper into the problem.

But if we discover the meaning of a certain difficulty, then in juxtaposition to that reality stands out in a more marked way as a spiritual counterfact. The futility of much of our prayers lies in the fact that we have a preconceived idea about how God should solve our problems. Prayer needs to be clearly understood as an endeavor to reach the point of beholding.

If we understand that our salvation lies in beholding divine reality right where the problem seems to be, then we do not have to wrestle with "shoulds"; we are oriented not toward what should or shouldn't be, but toward what is. God said to Moses, "I am what is."

Comment: Sometimes I feel frustrated when the demonstration is fuzzy.

Dr. Hora: The clarity of our demonstration is always in proportion to the clarity of our beholding. Can beholding be done?

Comment: No.

Dr. Hora: How can we do what cannot be done?

Comment: The desire to do is the fly in the ointment.

Dr. Hora: It indicates an operational approach to prayer.

Question: What was it in Job's consciousness that allowed him to behold something that made a radical change in his life?

Dr. Hora: The story of Job is this: First, he got into trouble due to self-righteous religiosity. He was a very religious and upright man, but he was proud of it. Then when he got into trouble he tried to solve his own problems through prayer. That did not work; it got worse. Then his friends came to visit him and he hoped they would solve his problem. And they did not solve it either because neither Job nor his friends nor anyone else could solve problems, not even God. Eventually, in his despair, he reached a point where he realized that not even God could solve his problems. Then he suddenly saw, and he said: "I have heard of thee by the hearing of the ear: but now mine eye seeth thee" (Job 42:5). He reached the point of beholding, and at that moment everything was healed.

Question: Can you throw more light on the issue of beholding?

Dr. Hora: It is mysterious because we are not accustomed to seeing anything but what is visible, and this requires us to look not upon the things which are seen, but upon the things which are not seen. "We look not at the things which are seen, but at the things which are not seen: for the things which are seen are temporal; but the things which are not seen are eternal" (II Corinthians 4:18).

As thou seest, so thou beest. What does the Buddha see? By looking at a statue of the Buddha, it is easy to see what he beholds and knows. He sees beauty, he sees harmony, he sees joy, he knows freedom, he knows peace, he knows truth, he knows perfection, he knows wisdom, he knows compassion. He sees everything that is real, everything that really *is.* He beholds reality and he is a manifestation of the reality he beholds. We become what we can really behold; therefore, every time we can fully behold something of reality, be it ever so little, something good must happen because reality is all good.

Dialogue No. 11

BEHOLDING THE GOOD

Question: Would you please clarify these three points: What is joy? What is excitement? What is a killjoy? I would also like to know how to be joyous all the time.

Dr. Hora: If we know *what*, we know *how*. Let us start by asking what is a joy killer? Is a killjoy a person? A killjoy is never a person. This is very important to know. What is the importance of this statement?

Comment: We cannot blame anybody.

Dr. Hora: Right. One of the most powerful killjoys is envy. Where there is envy in someone's consciousness, it will exert a powerful influence toward killing the joy in everybody who happens to be joyous. What other factors act as a killjoy besides envy?

Comment: Malice.

Dr. Hora: Pride, malice, ambition, guilt, what should be, and what shouldn't be. What do we call that? Willfulness and criticism. When such thoughts are present in someone's consciousness, then there are bad "vibes." Bad vibrations have the effect of killing the joy. It is possible to refuse to let our joy be killed. How do we do that?

Comment: It is important to know that our joy is from God.

Dr. Hora: It is good to know that God wants us to be joyous all the time. What is most helpful is this: that a killjoy is not a person. If we understand that, then nobody will be able to rob us of our joy. We will not be seeing envious people, we will not be seeing critical people, we will not be seeing ambitious people, we will not be seeing malicious people or nasty people. We will be seeing the error of envy, the error of malice, the error of ambition, the error of nastiness. Therefore, we will have no problems with people; we will be aware of the presence of error in the consciousness of some individuals. If the bath water is dirty, we don't throw out the child; we only spill out the water. If the diapers are wet, we don't throw away the baby; we discard the diapers. If we understand that the killjoy is not a person, then we are able to cope with the situation.

Now what is the difference between joy and excitement?

Comment: Joy is spiritual, excitement is personal.

Dr. Hora: Right. It is very easy to make the mistake of blaming someone for robbing us of our joy. But if we do that, there is nothing we can do about it. Unenlightened life is a constant fluctuation between excitement and depression.

Question: What is envy?

Dr. Hora: Envy is a belief that if we could have what others have, then we would be happy. One of the common bases for envy is the belief that the good of life is either a person, a place, or a thing. What is the good of life? What is really good?

Comment: The real good is the good of God.

Dr. Hora: That's right. The good of God is what?

Comment: PAGL.

Dr. Hora: That's right. Could you explain it?

Comment: The good of God is peace, assurance, gratitude, and love.

Dr. Hora: And joy and freedom. The good of God is intangible. This, of course, is hard to understand. How can something that we cannot touch, hold, or squeeze be good? How can something intangible, abstract, be good?

Comment: It cannot be destroyed.

Dr. Hora: Right. The Bible says: "Lay not up for yourselves treasures upon earth, where moth and rust doth corrupt, and where thieves break in and steal" (Matthew 6:19). If our good is intangible, we can never lose it, nobody can take it away, and it cannot disintegrate by itself. What is really good in life is intangible. It requires a certain amount of sophistication to realize that.

Comment: Lately, I have come to know more clearly that the good of God is the only thing that's really worthwhile, and I have been trying to appreciate it completely and eliminate everything else. This really requires a discipline of complete devotion because persons, places, and things keep intruding into consciousness. I want very much to be of one mind, and it is very difficult.

Dr. Hora: We could say that everybody is concerned with the good. We all want the good; we want to have nice things, beautiful cars, good clothes, money, and all sorts of things. And of course, there are people who have very bizarre ideas of what is good. Someone may think that being beaten with a whip is good. We could say that the craziness of the world consists of people seeking the good and not knowing what the real good is. To the unenlightened mind it is very difficult to conceive of the good exactly because it is intangible and not accessible to sensory validation. Is the good abstract or concrete?

Comment: Neither.

Dr. Hora: Could you explain that?

Comment: Something that's abstract is intellectual, and something that is concrete can be sensed. And the real is neither abstract nor concrete.

Dr. Hora: That's right.

Comment: Jesus said: "I am come that they may have life and have it more abundantly."

Dr. Hora: Yes. What did he mean by that? Convertible Cadillacs? What is the abundant life? It is the abundance of God's good, the intangible "stuff" which is real. The tangible is just illusion, and the intangible is the real.

Question: Would an enlightened person live in poverty?

Dr. Hora: Poverty is just as much an illusion as material riches. What is poverty? It is again a symptom of a false idea of what is good. Only if we think that material wealth is good, only then can we be poor. Anyone who knows what is really good can never be poor because the good of God is unlimited and available to all. If we keep in mind what is really good, everything in our lives will be turning out good. It is important to have the right concept and the right understanding of what the good really is. Our experience in this world is but a shadow of spiritual reality. In order for the shadow to be good, the substance has to be clearly defined. What is the substance of reality? It is the intangible good which is in our consciousness. If the substance is clearly defined in consciousness, it casts a perfect shadow and to us it appears as good experience in daily living. But we must not be interested in the good of God primarily in the hope that it will pay off in a material way, because we are not then sincere seekers of the truth, we have ulterior motives. But if we are sincerely interested in knowing the real good, then, of course, we will be blessed in every way, even in the material world, because the material world is the shadow of spiritual reality.

What happens when we have an abstract knowledge of the good of God? We become theologians.

Comment: It is like a filing cabinet of information.

Comment: What we just heard about the importance of having the good of God clearly defined in consciousness illuminates the importance of the "What?" question, because if we could know what joy was, or what anything was, then we could know how to get it. If something is clearly defined in consciousness, it already is ours in experience.

Dr. Hora: It makes no sense to ask "How?" until we have come to know "What?" The abstract knowledge of the good of God would make us theologians. Are theologians happy people? No, not at all. Just like any other scholarly people, they are living in their mental filing cabinets. The good of God is neither abstract nor concrete, it is neither tangible nor thinkable; it is real. Reality is neither abstract nor concrete, neither intellectual nor sensual, neither thinkable nor tangible; but it is knowable. The abstract we can think about, the tangible we can touch. But as far as reality is concerned, we can neither think about it nor touch it. The reality we can think about is not reality, it is but a thought about reality.

For instance, if we say God is truth, this is not the truth, it is only a statement about the truth. So it does not help to sit here and accumulate information about reality, this will not help. We are not here to accumulate information; we are here to *see.* Only that will help us; what we know *about* will help us little.

Question: Is seeing realization?

Dr. Hora: Yes. To see, to understand, to realize—these are synonyms. Most of the time we are just accumulating interesting information about reality; then we go home and somebody calls us on the telephone and we get depressed. Which proves that we have not learned anything.

Comment: Recently I was told that I needed to learn to meditate in order to go beyond intellectualism. I was shocked to hear that. The point was that I had to learn to commune with God. It was not sufficient to know about things but one had to have direct contact. This brought to light the issue of whether I am really interested in knowing God, or just in making impressions. And so there is some struggle going on within me.

Comment: My son was recently cured of asthma when I was sincerely endeavoring to understand Dr. Hora's principle of harmonious living which goes as follows: "Take no thought for what should be or what shouldn't be. Seek ye first to know the good of God which already is." This was a breakthrough in my life which brought many other blessings along with it. That principle seems to me miraculous, it was so helpful.

Dr. Hora: What does it mean to commune with God in meditation?

Comment: Communing with God is seeking the will of God.

Dr. Hora: The phrase "the will of God" may be meaningful to some, but not to others.

Question: Is communing with God clearly beholding some spiritual value?

Dr. Hora: Communing with God is beholding divine reality right where our problems seem to lie. What is beholding?

Comment: Seeing.

Dr. Hora: What kind of seeing?

Comment: Nonjudgmental and noncritical.

Dr. Hora: That is elementary. There is no prayer as long as there is criticism and judging. But what is the prayer of beholding—which we spoke of before, and which seems so mysterious to so many—about? When we want to pray the prayer of beholding, we must be willing to drop all imagination, fantasy, and worry. We must lose sight of the human picture altogether, and we must be willing to leave the situation completely in God's hands so that all thoughts of the human situation fall away. We are only aware that everything is under the control of divine Mind. We carefully refrain from thinking of how this Mind should do its job. That would already be a "should." So when we are able to erase the human situation from consciousness and find peace and assurance in the knowledge of God's absolute control, then we have beheld the Presence and there is PAGL. And when there is PAGL, we can be certain of the good unfolding.

But real PAGL can only come when we have succeeded in beholding the Presence right where problems seem to be rushing into thought. There is no problem that cannot be healed or solved or made to disappear, but we must not try to anticipate and imagine or outline how it should happen. "Trust in the Lord with all thine heart; and lean not unto thine own understanding" (Proverbs 3:5).

Dialogue No. 12

WHAT IS BEHOLDING?

Question: For the past few days I have been aware of an under-current of resentfulness, and I must admit that I am secretly enjoying it. And I wonder what it may lead to?

Dr. Hora: What is the difference between enjoying being resentful and enjoying scratching an itch?

Comment: None.

Dr. Hora: If we have an itch, it feels good to scratch it.

Comment: That's the quickest way to get rid of it.

Dr. Hora: I understand that New York City got into its financial mess by applying short-term solutions to long-term problems. When we are solving an itch by scratching it, we are doing the same.

Comment: The short-term solution to resentment is to vent our feelings.

Dr. Hora: There is a famous psychiatrist in New York who advises his patients to have a punching bag in their apartment and daily express their anger with the help of this implement. What is the solution to these problems? Enjoying resentful-ness, scratching our itches?

Question: Do you say we should ignore the itch?

Dr. Hora: We must neither scratch nor not scratch. Can that be done? When we scratch, we are involved with the itch. When we refrain from scratching, we are also involved with the itch. We must be involved with something else. What could we get involved with in order to neither scratch nor not scratch? The profitable way is to become involved with the thoughts of meaning. Never mind whether it itches or not, but what is the meaning of this phenomenon? What is it trying to say? Itching is not only an experience, it is a phenomenon. A phenomenon is a thought. It is never the body that itches. An itching body or a resentful person is a thought. What kind of thought is it? It is a thought about something that should be or should not be. And if we are more interested in coming to see the thought which underlies this phenomenon, we will be rewarded by a sudden discovery of the thought and at that moment the itch disappears, or the resentment vanishes. And then we can ask the question: "But what is what really *is?*"

Question: The itch and the resentment disappear just by understanding the thought it expresses?

Dr. Hora: Yes, because we have translated the phenomenon into its constituent thought.

Comment: That means that there is no more need for the phenomenon to call attention to the thought.

Dr. Hora: When we ask the question: "What is the meaning of what seems to be?" we are seeking the thought behind the phenomenon. In other words, we are converting the symptom into the thought.

Comment: Because it was a thought initially and we just expose it.

Dr. Hora: Right. If we are halfway enlightened, we can do this. We can transmute a symptom into a thought. Jesus was so enlightened that he could transmute thoughts into objects. All he had to do was say: "We need bread and fish for five thousand people; I have this thought of infinite abundance of supply." And immediately the fish and the bread appeared in material form. If a material form can be translated into a thought which is formlessness, then formlessness can be translated into form. What is thought? Thought is energy. Who knows the second law of thermodynamics?

Comment: Energy can neither be created nor destroyed.

Dr. Hora: Right. It is continually transmuted into other forms of energy. When a thought becomes an itch or a boil or an emotion, then the thought, which is energy, has been transmuted into form. The Zen Master says: "Form is formlessness and formlessness is form."

In one of our groups, one lady recently had a growth on her face. This growth suddenly disappeared on Thanksgiving Day when the thought of family strife was healed. What happened? Energy in the form of a growth was transmuted into a thought, and the thought was then healed with the help of realized truth.

Jesus was able to work it in both directions. He could transform thoughts into matter. He could walk on water. To him water was not a material substance; it was a form of energy made of thought. And his own body was nothing concrete or material, but a form of energy.

Since we are only semi-enlightened, we will be very grateful if we can transmute anger, resentfulness, itching, or ambition into its constituent thought, and then we can get rid of it. Now we can ask: "If thought is energy (and we know that there are valid thoughts and invalid thoughts), what is the relationship between these two types of thoughts?" The previous example of the healing of the growth on the lady's face illustrates the relationship between the valid and the invalid thoughts. When the valid thought—truth and love—is realized in consciousness, the invalid thought is abolished.

Question: Was it really energy?

Dr. Hora: Of course not. True energy cannot be destroyed. It is pseudo-energy, which seems to be but is not. Whatever is not divine is the counterfeit of the divine.

Question: How can nothing have the power to take form? Isn't energy needed for that?

Dr. Hora: The Zen Master says: "Form is formlessness and formlessness is form."

Question: Where does energy come in here?

Dr. Hora: He doesn't say, "formlessness causes form to be," he says "form is formlessness and formlessness is form," which means it is nothing, it is just appearance. Whether it appears as a thought or as a tumor, it is still nothing, it just seems to be. Only divine reality is substantial and real power. So, in order to bring divine energy to bear on pseudo-energy, we need to understand both. If we are willing to become more interested in the meaning of a symptom than in the symptom itself, then we are transcending it. We are not getting involved with it, but we go beyond it; and the meaning, which is the thought underlying the symptom, reveals itself to us. And then we can be healed.

Question: What determines, at that point, whether we are healed or not?

Dr. Hora: What determines it is whether we have sufficient acquaintance with real energy.

Comment: Sometimes the grace of God can reach us and heal us even without our having come to understand the meaning of our problem.

Dr. Hora: Of course, we can be very grateful for such spontaneous healings; but if we have not understood the problem, it may return. Problems, whether physical, emotional, interpersonal, economic, or social, are just thoughts. Buddha said: "We are what we think, having become what we thought."

Question: Doesn't that negate Genesis?

Dr. Hora: Buddha was talking about man the phenomenon, not of man the noumenon. He was talking about man as he appears to be. Buddha's saying is not quite correct, for we have become what we have accepted of what others have thought of us. Most of what we appear to be today is just a transmutation of those thought energies that others have thought about us in our childhood.

Comment: Which we have accepted as our own thoughts.

Dr. Hora: Right. And which we cling to, to our detriment. If we knew what we really are, we would disappear. Whenever the truth comes into contact with what seems to be, that which seems to be disappears. Just as whenever light comes into contact with darkness, darkness disappears.

All problems are psychological and all solutions are spiritual. This makes it very important to learn to pray the prayer of beholding. What is beholding? Beholding is the most fantastic thing that man can possibly understand. It is the faculty to be aware of the unthinkable, to see the invisible, and to know the inconceivable and unimaginable. Beholding is a great gift of God. The Apostle Paul wrote: "We look not at the things which are seen, but at the things which are not seen: for the things which are seen are temporal; but the things which are not seen are eternal" (II Corinthians 4:18). How in the world can we look upon things which are not seen?

Comment: He also said: "The invisible things of him from

the creation of the world are clearly seen, being understood by the things that are made, even his eternal power and Godhead" (Romans 1:20).

Dr. Hora: Beholding is a faculty which we all have and which makes it possible to know, to become aware of, the invisible and inconceivable. The good of God is invisible and inconceivable, and yet we can behold it in a meaningful way. Every time we succeed, a healing takes place. Whatever problems may be disturbing us at that moment, they will be healed. So we speak about the prayer of beholding, and we fervently desire to develop this faculty to the utmost. That can be done through meditation, carefully guarding against slipping into fantasies and falling asleep.

Dialogue No. 13

BEYOND RELIGION

Comment: I had an interesting experience this weekend. I found myself complaining, and when it was over I realized how self-indulgent it was. I realized the gulf between saying things about God and actually basing one's life on God. I was unwilling to forego the pleasures of life. I felt like complaining and I did.

Comment: I was thinking the very same thing today, that for years I have been sitting and hearing and thinking and trying hard to live according to what we learn here. And it seems to me that it wasn't till about two weeks ago that I ever really made a sincere effort to put God first. Something happened lately where I can see the gulf between talking about it, making it sound really nice, and making it a principle by which to live.

Comment: The passage of Scripture that came to me was: "Thou shalt have no other gods before me."

Comment: To complain or to refrain from complaining—isn't that the same thing?

Dr. Hora: What is the solution then?

Comment: We have to love the Lord, our God, with all our heart, and with all our soul, and with all our might. ("And thou shalt love the Lord thy God with all thine heart, and with all thy soul, and with all thy might," Deuteronomy 6:5.)

Comment: Yes, I had refrained from complaining for such a long time, that it was a pleasure to complain.

Dr. Hora: When we consider the first commandment, doesn't it sound like a "should"? Doesn't it seem very strenuous? It is as if someone were requiring us to make an effort to love God. Doesn't it contradict everything we were saying about what should be and shouldn't be?

Comment: No. Because it is what *is*. It is the truth, which we need. God is what is and we are what we are. That's not very clear but there doesn't seem to be any other alternative.

Comment: I think of the Ten Commandments now as rather a description of what *is*. They don't say what we should do; but if we live in this manner, then we are in harmony.

Dr. Hora: What happens to us when the "shoulds" disappear from our thinking, or from the Bible? There are many "shoulds" and "should nots" in the Bible, but as long as we live by these "shoulds," we are only religious. When we become enlightened, all the "shoulds" disappear. What is left?

Comment: Is is left.

Dr. Hora: So how does an enlightened individual read the Commandments?

Comment: If you really understand, then you read the first commandment in this manner: Thou hast no choice but to love the Lord thy God with all thine heart, and with all thine soul, and with all thy might.

Comment: It could perhaps be described as striving to love God.

Dr. Hora: If we strive, then it is strenuous.

Comment: What if we would say "Blessed are you if you love the Lord thy God"?

Dr. Hora: That's a little better.

Comment: What about saying "Because God is the substance of our being, we can love"?

Comment: If we understood that God is love, then we would love God.

Comment: And if we understood that we and our Father are one.

Dr. Hora: Religion is really based on the assumption that there is an enormous gap between God and man. And man has to struggle all his life somehow, through bribery, good behavior, ritualistic performances, good works, charity, and all sorts of rigamarole, to get in touch with this distant God. The Bible is full of recommendations on how to do this, what we should do and what we shouldn't do. Little wonder that religion is strenuous; the religious life is really tough and many people are put off by it. But last week we were talking about a different kind of prayer.

Comment: First we have to realize who we are.

Dr. Hora: Let us see what happens to the First Commandment when we realize that we are emanations of God.

Comment: Then we are love.

Comment: Then we don't need the First Commandment.

Dr. Hora: We could say: An emanation of God is naturally loving with all his heart, and with all his soul, and with all his might. He is naturally loving because love is one of the basic attributes of God. There is no effort involved whatsoever, only a recognition of what already is.

In what way would it be helpful to all of us to really live according to what we are learning here, instead of just trying to occasionally? It would never occur to us to complain or gossip or hate or envy or fear or suffer or be jealous or competitive, because these ideas are totally alien to an emanation of God. It would be impossible for us to have a spoiled weekend, or anything else. It would not be an effort to live up to these principles we are learning about here because we *are* these principles. So the question "How to?" is irrelevant and misleading. There is only *is;* perfect spiritual being is all there is. Whatever does not comprise the attributes of God is no part of an emanation of God. Can you imagine a sunbeam which would include in itself darkness? In a sunbeam there can be no darkness at all because the sun does not contain any darkness. And a sunbeam comprises all the qualities of the sun. And if man is an emanation of God, then he is made up of all the attributes of God and nothing else. Can you imagine God ever complaining? Even though in the Old Testament there are intimations of that. The revolutionary idea is that man is not a separate entity struggling to establish contact with a distant, faraway God.

Comment: When this emanation finds itself complaining, isn't that a contradiction? I lived on a hillside all summer, and when I had to walk up the hill many times a day, I felt like complaining about being tired. There is no lack of energy in God, but my legs were tired.

Dr. Hora: An emanation of God lives in divine reality where everything is timeless, infinite, immortal, and perfect.

Question: If we are in this world but not of it, aren't we subject to the conditions of this world?

Dr. Hora: In space there is absolute darkness, the sunbeam travels through space but the darkness does not know about it. It is a little difficult to fully realize our oneness with God as emanations of divine Mind because it doesn't seem that way. Everything seems to conspire to tell us that it is not so, that we are just individual little creatures running around like insects on the face of the earth.

It is interesting that the word "religion" comes from the Latin *religio,* which means to re-establish the tie. If we are going to re-establish something, it must mean that it was broken at one time. The idea is that, perhaps before we were born, we may have been at one with God, but after birth the umbilical cord became severed and we are now cast adrift in the universe without any contact with God. It seems that way to the eyes. Everything points to this. So it is illogical to claim that man is an emanation of divine mind. What justification is there to make such a claim? Isn't it preposterous? How could we substantiate the validity of such a claim that man is an emanation of the divine mind? Unless we can substantiate this claim, it is a lie.

Comment: Our lives and our healing experiences can testify to the validity of this claim.

Comment: If I examine the improvements in my life, I see that they are not accomplishments but the result of letting go of false perceptions, which indicates to me that what we are talking about really is, that it is not just a technique or super-stition.

Comment: Being religious is based on cause-and-effect think-ing. It is easy to slip into that. For instance, we rely on God, therefore something good will happen. That's a dangerous mistake.

Dr. Hora: It is not dangerous, but neither is it liberating and enlightening.

Comment: We can also prove the truth by understanding the consequences of thinking in the opposite direction, by the troubles we get into. And, therefore, this type of thinking, which helps us overcome these troubles, is probably valid.

Dr. Hora: This is called *post hoc ergo propter hoc* reasoning. What does that mean?

Comment: If something happens after something, then it happens because of it.

Dr. Hora: But that's not proof, we have long discarded cause-and-effect thinking.

Comment: It seems we have to come to know what the essence of God is and, once we know what it is, to see it in ourselves as individuals. With this we will find that we are made of the same stuff, the same essence.

Dr. Hora: You are coming very close. What we must start out with is to ask: "What is the essence of man?" According to appearances, the essence of man is flesh, blood, bones, organs, and so on. But there is also a mysterious aspect of man which is unique to man, and that is called consciousness. And as we study man we become more and more impressed by the absolute supremacy of consciousness, up to the point where we come to realize that consciousness is all that really matters. Man without consciousness is nothing, just decaying organic matter. So what really makes the difference is consciousness.

Comment: A corpse without consciousness is really dead, and would be pronounced dead by medical authorities.

Dr. Hora: But there is really no such thing as death.

Comment: Because consciousness doesn't die.

Comment: Only appearance disappears.

Comment: That's very helpful, because consciousness is not something we can argue about.

Dr. Hora: Last week I asked a physician: "Where do your intelligent ideas come from?" And he promptly answered: "From my forebrain." So I asked him: "Where does your forebrain get it from?" He didn't know. Then I asked him: "Have you ever heard of God?" He said: "I am not religious." So if we consider it carefully, we find that man is consciousness. What is consciousness?

Comment: It is an awareness which allows us to know what thoughts are present.

Dr. Hora: Right. It is a quality of our being which makes it possible for us to be aware of ideas. Has anyone here ever become aware of an idea? An original, intelligent, creative idea? I am sure everyone has. And where did it come from? The forebrain cannot produce an intelligent idea. Consciousness does not produce ideas, just as a radio does not produce music, it receives the music. Man receives ideas. The flower receives the sunbeam directly from the sun. The sun is the source of that vital energy which makes the flower blossom. There is a direct connection between the sun and the flower. Similarly, there is a direct connection between God and that consciousness which man is. Man cannot reach up to God, man is connected with God and inseparable from God as consciousness. Another name for God is Cosmic Consciousness.

Question: Where do invalid thoughts come from?

Dr. Hora: From their source. What is the source of invalid thoughts? The "sea of mental garbage," the noosphere.

Question: Where did the "sea of mental garbage" come from?

Dr. Hora: Where did two and two is five come from?

Comment: The same place as the "sea of mental garbage."

Question: How do we account for all the garbage in our consciousness? How does it enter there and from where?

Dr. Hora: How does darkness enter a sunbeam?

Comment: Well, it doesn't.

Dr. Hora: Right. How does garbage enter a divine emanation?

Comment: It really doesn't. It just seems to.

Dr. Hora: What is the first intelligent question?

Answer: What is the meaning of what seems to be?

Dr. Hora: Right. Those of you who are Bible scholars know the answer to this question: What is the meaning of the two accounts of creation in the Book of Genesis? This has stymied theologians through the ages. They could not explain the mystery of two contradictory accounts of creation. And now that we have the benefit of understanding the two intelligent questions, it has become very clear to us. One is the account of what really is, the other is the account of things that seem to be. So man is an individualized divine consciousness and is constantly being bombarded by intelligent ideas, vital forces, love, energy, and everything good from God. The more clearly we can see ourselves as emanations of God, the more enlightened and effective our prayers will be. And to live according to the principles we are learning about will not be such an arduous task as it hitherto appeared to be, but it will be a spontaneous and most natural way to be. "My Father worketh hitherto, and I work" (John 5:17).

Let us return to the issue of tiredness which was raised earlier. Today a lady complained extensively about severe muscle pains which developed after she has "abused herself" during house cleaning. A religious person would naturally abuse himself in cleaning the house. But an enlightened individual would clean the house in such a way as to be useful. What is the difference between self-abuse and usefulness?

Comment: The direction. One is self-confirming, the other helpful.

Question: Do self-confirmatory thoughts also come from the "sea of mental garbage"?

Dr. Hora: What do we do when we are engaged in self-confirmatory thinking? We are trying to reassure ourselves that our ignorance is valid. If we do not have the right understanding, walking up a hill, vacuuming the rug, cooking a meal, writing a paper, can be forms of self-abuse. You hear people say: "I worked so hard, I am sick." Or: "I got myself exhausted." Self-abuse, self-pampering and self-indulgence are all the same. It is having the wrong perspective on oneself outside of the context of divine reality. When we can maintain a clear idea of ourselves within the context of our at-one-ment with God, then we are not abusing ourselves, we are being useful, and perhaps we even accomplish more without any ill effect. This has very practical application in everyday life. The right understanding of what really is will make a radical difference in our experiences. Clearly, it is not just theological fancy talk that we are engaged in, but it has practical applicability, not only on weekends but always.

Dialogue No. 14

SYMBOLIC STRUCTURES

Question: Would you please talk tonight about the meaning of Christmas? I would like to have a clear view of the celebrating that goes on and its relevancy to Christmas.

Dr. Hora: We could start out then by asking the following question: "Is Christmas a Christian holiday, or is it a Jewish one?"

Comment: I was thinking of Christmas, not as a Christian holiday or a Jewish holiday, but as a time when we think of the Christ, not necessarily Jesus Christ. In that sense, I would say every day could be Christmas.

Dr. Hora: Two thousand years ago a Jewish boy was born to a Jewish mother and this occasion has become a Christian holiday. What are we to make of that?

Comment: It is a new consciousness, a new way of thinking.

Dr. Hora: Has Jesus presented us with a philosophy? Has he presented us with a religion?

Comment: No.

Dr. Hora: What did Jesus give us?

Comment: Liberation.

Dr. Hora: What kind of liberation?

Comment: Liberation from a sense of personhood.

Dr. Hora: Could you explain that?

Comment: If you are a person, there is the self and others.

Dr. Hora: Is there a passage in the Bible that is relevant to this?

Comment: "There is neither Jew nor Greek, there is neither bond nor free, there is neither male nor female: for ye are all one in Christ Jesus" (Galatians 3:28).

Dr. Hora: Isn't that a revolutionary statement? It suddenly erases all the polarizations which people tend to develop in their thinking. Someone could say, however, that you cannot just overlook the differences. What happens to our differences in Christ Jesus? What does it mean in Christ Jesus?

Comment: Would our differences be like snowflakes, which are all the same yet unique?

Dr. Hora: Right. Our unique individuality is not erased, but it comes into its own in a more distinctive and more beautiful way, and yet we are all one. In what way are we all one? And what practical relevancy does this idea have?

Comment: It means that we do not have to establish ourselves in opposition to each other by claiming differences between each other.

Dr. Hora: I know a lady who had a lifelong problem in that she could only read backwards; she could not read normally and, consequently, she read very little. This was a great mystery to the various specialists whom she consulted; no underlying cause could be found. They examined her eyes and her nervous system; all sorts of tests were made, but it remained a mystery. It was called a reading disability. When we were talking about it, it suddenly became clear that she did not have a reading problem; she was just contrary. The entire syndrome was an expression of her contrariness, the purpose of which was to define herself as a person in her own right in opposition to other people. This came to her as a great surprise, and the sudden recognition of its truth resulted in an instantaneous healing.

Another idea is that we all have minds of our own and therefore we have to live in contention with others. Personal minds cherish personal opinions, and these opinions are at odds with each other. Jesus said that we are all one. What does that mean? He said, in fact, that though we may be unique individualities, we all have one mind. How is that possible with so much dissension in the world? How can there be just one mind? If there were just one mind, wouldn't we all be of one mind? Wouldn't then everybody agree with everybody else? How can there be just one mind?

Comment: Dissension comes from opinions, Mind has no opinions.

Dr. Hora: What does Mind have?

Comment: Ideas.

Dr. Hora: Does that have any practical value? One of the practical aspects of this truth is that, if we want to understand something, we must refrain from thinking. Thinking interferes with understanding, unfolding. How does understanding come about?

Comment: It obtains.

Dr. Hora: What does that mean? The word "obtain" is a peculiar word. To obtain means to receive. It refers to some insight or realization, an event which happens in consciousness. When we obtain something, we are getting an invisible gift from an invisible source.

What would happen if the world would suddenly understand that God is the Mind of the universe, and that besides this Mind there is no other Mind? Would that have practical consequences?

Comment: Self-confirmation would come to a stop.

Comment: All conflicts would cease.

Dr. Hora: Yes. All conflicts and fears would vanish. And what then?

Comment: People would turn their attention to seeing what really is and being what they really are.

Dr. Hora: There would be harmonious participation in the good of God. Universal and permanent Christmas. And all the wisdom which is needed at any moment in life and is adequate to any task at hand would be available. There would be no contention, no rivalry; there would be no self-confirmatory behavior; there would be no one-up-manship; there would be no self-effacing behavior. There would be none of these distortions of life which we see and experience so often. Everyone would be intelligent and peaceful and responsive, alert and loving.

Comment: "Peace on earth, good will to men."

Dr. Hora: The right understanding—even just an admission without understanding, just a willingness to consider the possibility that there is only one mind—would immediately bring a great deal of peace, harmony, and healing into our experience, so powerful is the truth. And any time we are involved in a controversy or unpleasant experience with people, or confronted with decisions or plans that seem to be anxiety producing, all we need to do is to become very quiet and mentally acknowledge that there is only one Mind and that this Mind has all the answers. And if we will only be quiet and let it, we will be able to respond adequately to whatever situation may arise. In order for that to take place, there is only one requirement: not to try to figure out solutions to our own problems. As long as we try to figure things out ourselves, our affirmations are not sincere. When we do that, we deny the existence of God—the one Mind which is the source of all intelligent ideas.

Question: What exactly is love in a practical sense?

Dr. Hora: Love is divine Mind's response to manifest needs.

Question: What is the brain?

Dr. Hora: The brain is the same as any other organ of the body. What are the eyes or the ears?

Comment: They are material counterfeits of the faculties of hearing, seeing, thinking.

Dr. Hora: They are symbolic structures representing certain faculties of Mind. For instance, the eyes are symbolic structures representing the faculty of sight. The eyes cannot see; sight sees. We do not see because we have eyes; we have eyes because we see. Similarly, the brain is a symbolic structure indicating that there is such a thing as mind. We do not have mind because we have a brain, but we have a brain because there is mind. What is a symbolic structure?

Comment: The outward manifestation of a thought or an idea or a faculty.

Dr. Hora: That's right.

Comment: The formless appearing as form.

Dr. Hora: When a sculptor has an idea—for instance *Bird in Flight* by Brancusi—this idea is expressed as sculpture in a certain form, and that form becomes a symbolic structure indicating the idea. But the real issue is the idea. Symbolic structures can be multiplied, but the idea is one.

Question: Is the idea spiritual?

Dr. Hora: All right ideas are spiritual. What are wrong ideas?

Comment: They are garbage, or error.

Question: What is the meaning of having two eyes, two ears, two brain lobes, or two nostrils?

Dr. Hora: We can only speculate that the symbolic structures represent reality in terms of dualism. It reminds us of the serpent's claim whispered to Adam and Eve: "In the day ye eat thereof [the forbidden fruit], Then your eyes shall be opened, and ye shall be as gods, knowing good and evil" (Genesis 3:5). God knows nothing of good and evil; God is one and God *is* good.

Question: When you say that we mentally acknowledge the goodness and allness of God, what is it or who is it that does the acknowledging? Is it the brain?

Dr. Hora: It has nothing to do with the brain, just as seeing has nothing to do with the eyes. The brain can do nothing by itself.

Question: What about seeing having to do with the brain?

Dr. Hora: That is what medical science believes. If there is damage to the brain, there is no seeing; when there is damage to the eyes, there is no experience of sight. However, it is not that simple. There is sight even if man does not see. Now the question was, when we acknowledge the truth, who does it? Is it the brain that does it?

Comment: The spirit acknowledges the spirit.

Dr. Hora: When the truth is being acknowledged or sought in prayer or in an endeavor to behold, it is consciousness that does it, and it takes place in consciousness. When we say "we" or "I," it can be the material counterfeit symbolic structure because the whole person is a symbolic structure counterfeiting the real man. But if we are seeking the truth, then it is an entirely different individuality that is involved; then it is the spiritual being who is turning his attention to the truth. The Bible says: "The Spirit itself beareth witness with our spirit, that we are the children of God" (Romans 8:16). A good example of this is if we say that two and two is four and then say that two and two is five, the difference on the surface does not seem so very striking; but, in fact, there is a radical difference. If we are involved with the truth, we are real. If we are involved with error, we are nothing. We are what we know.

If we know something that does not exist, then we do not exist. But if we know what really is, we really are.

Comment: That part of us which knows evil and confusion does not exist.

Dr. Hora: Right.

Comment: The prayer that always helps me is this: "Let this mind be in you, which was also in Christ Jesus" (Philippians 2:5).

Dr. Hora: That's a very good prayer. We are either on the beam or off the beam. When we are off the beam, we are nothing, or as the Bible says, "a thing of naught." The Zen Master says: "The thinker and the thought are one." If the thoughts are invalid, then the thinker is an invalid phenomenon; he does not really exist. The Bible says: "God is love; and he that dwelleth in love dwelleth in God, and God in him" (1 John 4:16). So when we are oriented toward becoming real, realizing our true self-identity, we are involved with love and its expression. Love expresses itself in being responsive to manifest needs, and we are then dwelling in love. That means we are dwelling in God and God is dwelling in us. We are then at-one with God. That is the best way to stay on the beam all the time—to see ourselves as need-suppliers.

Dialogue No. 15

WHAT IS A HEALING?

Question: "Would you please explain the difference between a healing and just a normal repair of the body? We know that the body tends to repair itself.

Dr. Hora: Let us then consider the difference between healing, cure, and spontaneous repair. Do doctors heal?

Comment: No.

Dr. Hora: There is a famous saying in Latin which goes like this: *Medicus curat, natura sanat* (doctors treat and nature heals). That, of course, is an old-fashioned saying and is not quite accurate because it was based on superficial observation. Suppose someone has the flu. He may do nothing about it and it may go away. Or he may do something about it— apply various remedies by himself or on a doctor's prescription—and it still may go away. Or he can try to understand the meaning of that experience and then correct the underlying mental error and be healed. If we want to understand the difference between a cure and what is called a spontaneous remission and a healing, let us consider the following. If there is a spontaneous remission, who or what is doing it?

Comment: One erroneous idea is replaced by another idea.

Dr. Hora: In the late nineteenth century there was a physician in Vienna by the name of Wagner-Jaureg who invented a cure for syphilis. This cure consisted of inoculating syphilitic patients with malaria. The idea behind this method was that a lesser illness would successfully replace a more serious illness. This is an interesting historical fact because it throws light, to some extent, on the mystery of disease and what is involved in spontaneous remissions, or even medical cures.

We mentioned three modes of liberation from sickness: spontaneous remission, medical cure, and spiritual healing. Is there a fourth way? Yes, there is a fourth way, and it is called faith healing. What is faith healing? Having faith in the power of God, either directly or through a mediator. This kind of faith is a form of religious hypnotism or auto-suggestion. It can bring about relief of a problem. How is it possible that having faith either in a person or an idea could relieve us of an illness, actually make us feel good? What does that say about the nature of illness?

Comment: It is mental.

Dr. Hora: Right. But suppose it is arthritis?

Comment: It is still mental.

Dr. Hora: Yes, the physical is mental. Isn't it interesting? So what is really needed is an alteration of consciousness in every case. It can happen spontaneously; it can happen through faith in a doctor, a drug, mud baths, climate, or vegetables. Whatever can induce a change in consciousness may have a beneficial effect on a physical condition. Unfortunately, in all these situations we remain ignorant.

Question: Would you say that this is exchanging a bad dream with a good dream?

Dr. Hora: Yes, a bad dream of illness and suffering for a better dream of something else. But when it comes to real healing, something radical has taken place in consciousness. Not only do we have to understand the meaning of our suffering, but also the spiritual counterfact to that particular idea. And when that happens, something more takes place than a relief of symptoms. What is it that happens?

Comment: We are able to see something and understand something that previously we did not. And that's the great difference.

Dr. Hora: Now what's so great about seeing something we have not seen previously?

Comment: If it is reality that we are discerning, that makes us whole.

Dr. Hora: Oddly enough, sometimes it happens that people who were healed in this manner clearly express great joy and gratitude over having been sick. Ordinarily, people feel sorry for themselves for having suffered; but in cases where real healing takes place, there is a sense of gratitude for the experience because it has brought about a realization which is of great value to the individual. Once we understand the true nature of healing, there is a valuable lesson in it for us all. If we have a problem, we do not have to seek fast relief, or even a quick healing to get rid of the problem as soon as possible. We may embrace the problem and say the same thing that Jacob said. What did Jacob say when he wrestled with the angel (his problem)?

Comment: "I will not let thee go, except thou bless me" (Genesis 32:26).

Dr. Hora: If we quickly get rid of a problem and find relief, we are missing an opportunity to learn something vitally important.

Occasionally we have spoken of hypnotism. What role does hypnotism play in illness and the cure of illness?

Comment: Illness itself can be hypnotic. We can become hypnotized by the picture that the symptom presents, or the picture that the cure presents, or the pleasure of discussing it with a neighbor. We can be quite taken up by that.

Comment: We are hypnotized most of the time.

Dr. Hora: What is the state of hypnotism?

Comment: It is sleep.

Dr. Hora: The nature of a cure is changing the dream from an unpleasant one to a more acceptable one. All forms of cure and spontaneous remission are just a shift in the hypnotic state from a negative one to a more acceptable one. But in healing based on spiritual understanding the hypnotic spell is broken and there is a certain degree of awakening. On that basis, we can see the qualitative difference between spiritual realization and any other form of relief which we may avail ourselves of in case of need. So it is qualitatively and radically different.

Someone else mentioned here that cures are not lasting. As a matter of fact, the more quickly we get cured of a problem, the easier it is to get it back again. There are some people who suffer from recurrent conditions of one type or another. How do we understand this phenomenon of recurrence? If we allow ourselves to be hypnotized once, it is much easier to become hypnotized the second time; and the more often it is repeated, the more susceptible we become. This is called suggestibility. But if we are truly healed of a problem, we will never get it back. It is permanent because the hypnotism has been broken.

Comment: The mode of being-in-the-world changes and our character undergoes a transformation. That's the greatest healing.

Question: What is the difference between hypnotism and a mantra used in meditation?

Dr. Hora: Well, one can easily misuse a mantra, even to put oneself to sleep.

Question: Can't a mantra be used for faith healing?

Dr. Hora: Yes, we can make almost anything we want of it, but that is not the original purpose of the mantra. The purpose of the mantra is to keep thought in a certain direction without getting distracted. It is important to know the difference between waking up and changing a dream. The aim of life is, of course, to wake up completely.

One of the greatest temptations of life is to influence people. Suppose we don't want someone to find something. If we think hard, he may get confused and he wouldn't be able to find it. Sometimes we can seemingly exert this kind of power and hypnotize or confuse people, distract them. If we succeed in this kind of activity, it is dangerous because we get to liking it and we may begin to believe in personal mind-power. There are people who love to be hypnotists.

Question: Was that one of the temptations which Jesus overcame?

Dr. Hora: Yes. He refused the temptation of personal mind-power. Our culture naturally values the idea. It is called executive ability, leadership quality, charisma, command presence, managerial skill.

The enlightened man does not think about what should be and what should not be, he is conscious of the unfolding presence of God's good. And then there is no confusion. Every step of the way is a marvel of harmonious movement from good to better.

What is a Healing?

It is not necessary to influence and it is not necessary to think about what should be or shouldn't be. The good already is. All that is necessary is to behold it, to discern it, to acknowledge it. And if we rest in that knowledge, it will come into view.

Dialogue No. 16

FREEDOM AND JOY

Question: Would you please talk to us about intercessory prayer?

Dr. Hora: In order to understand intercessory prayer, we must first understand hypnotism. What is hypnotism?

Comment: It is the power of suggestion.

Dr. Hora: Hypnotism is a belief in and a susceptibility to being mentally influenced. People are constantly exerting influence upon one another. Enlightened people are exerting beneficial influence on everyone around them. The sicker and more ignorant someone is, the more harmful mental influence he is radiating. In popular language this is referred to as "vibes," or vibrations.

The essence of intercessory prayer is healing ourselves of the effects of the bad vibes we receive from contact with others. How is that possible? In what way will it benefit another if we heal ourselves of the effects of his bad vibrations?

Comment: Because we do that by clarifying the truth to ourselves about the other individual so that the mistaken idea of the other individual is erased.

Dr. Hora: Isn't it interesting that the right understanding of hypnotism can help us to practice intercessory prayer in an effective way?

Question: You mean that under ordinary circumstances we are hypnotized by the vibrations of other people?

Dr. Hora: Yes. Every evil, jealous, envious, competitive, hostile, greedy, malicious, fearful thought which we entertain has a radiancy of its own which communicates itself through subliminal channels to everyone around us; if we come into contact with someone who is involved with this kind of thinking, we become affected by it without realizing it.

Comment: I know that if I entertain some of these thoughts and come into the presence of someone with similar thoughts, my thoughts go wild.

Dr. Hora: Yes. You have just described the phenomenon of potentiation. When two people who are bitter, for instance, come together, there is an increase of bitterness. Would you all like to know how to be immune to hypnotism? What is the first thing that happens when we get hypnotized? The first sign is the loss of joy. The normal condition of man is to be joyful. Isn't that interesting?

Comment: It's fantastic, I never knew that.

Comment: It would seem that we are born hypnotized.

Dr. Hora: The vast majority of people are living their lives in a state of mesmerism. They do not even know what it means to be awake. To be awake means joy.

Comment: We don't even know that we are asleep.

Dr. Hora: We have to understand that joy is a God-given gift to man, and we have the right not to permit ourselves to become joyless. The moment we catch ourselves joyless, that is a sign that we are hypnotized. And what do we do then?

Comment: We complain.

Dr. Hora: What happens if we complain? We sink deeper into a state of hypnotism. Therefore, complaining is not advisable. We must rouse ourselves, take a vigorous stand, shake off the hypnotism as illegitimate, and remind ourselves that God is joy and that his image and likeness has to manifest joy and freedom. When we are hypnotized, we are captives of someone else's mood. So joy is the first thing we must struggle to recapture, as well as the freedom from being influenced by the thoughts and moods of others. We can do this through prayer and the knowledge that it is the will of God that we be free and joyous always.

We have the power to reject mesmerism, hypnotism, and claim our God-given right to freedom and joy. Every time we succeed in this we are blessed and others are blessed also, particularly those that have induced our hypnotic state, for we are breaking the spell. When the spell is broken, then the one who was the source of the hypnotism is also benefited.

Comment: Because if they have seen you react differently

than they have expected, that wakes them up.

Dr. Hora: Interestingly enough, visual contact is not essential. Suppose we are hypnotized by an evil report which came to us from a hundred or a thousand miles away, and we get depressed. Depression is joylessness. It is a state of hypnotism. If we rouse ourselves out of that hypnotism and establish our God-given position of freedom and joy, an individual a thousand miles away may benefit by what we did for ourselves. How is that possible?

Comment: In divine reality there is no time and space.

Dr. Hora: God is simultaneously present everywhere, and every time we heal ourselves, the source of our hypnotism is affected favorably.

Dialogue No. 17
SAFETY

Comment: I feel very upset today because a friend of mine has been a victim of rape.

Dr. Hora: So ask a question.

Question: What do I need to know about this problem?

Dr. Hora: What do you need to know in order to get raped? Or to make sure that you don't get raped? There are only two ways to get raped: by wanting to or by not wanting to.

Comment: What I would like to know also is how to be helpful to my friend in comforting her.

Dr. Hora: Then the question you are asking is: "What would be the right attitude to take toward a victim of crime, notably a sex crime?" What do we mean by saying that the only way to get raped is by wanting to or not wanting to?

Comment: Because in either case we are mentally involved with the idea of victimization. Nothing comes into experience uninvited.

Dr. Hora: Yes. But that does not mean necessarily that we are asking to be raped. There is a lot of talk nowadays about rape, especially among women liberationists; books are being written about it, it is being discussed on television, and it is filling the minds of people with fear and mental preoccupation. If we are not aware of the dynamism which underlies our experiences, then we have no answers. We live in a certain cultural climate, we are being bombarded with ideas about various forms of crime, diseases, surgical operations, and all sorts of problems. These ideas fill our consciousness and we either want them or don't want them. Or we may say: "I don't want to think about them. I don't want to know about them." And the more we try not to know about them, to protect ourselves against them, to run away from them, the more we are inviting them. It is interesting that for a long time women were being accused of inviting rape, and there was a callous attitude on the part of the police and the courts toward women who were raped. Somehow there was always a suspicion that the victim had something to do with this experience. And this was being misinterpreted as wanting it. Not many people understand that not wanting has the same attracting influence as wanting. Therefore, the victim cannot be blamed for what happened to her, neither is she completely innocent. It is important not to laugh it off when we say that there are only two ways to get raped: by wanting to or by not wanting to. This needs to be thoroughly understood because then there is the possibility of protection. Of course, this is not only a female problem, it is a problem of victimology in general.

Did you ever hear of victimology? It is a new science, the science of victomology. It is an important science because it may lead to the discovery of God. How can it lead to the discovery of God?

Comment: If it exposes the fact that nothing comes into one's experience uninvited, that will reveal the importance of understanding something rather than just changing the external circumstances.

Dr. Hora: If the science of victimology would explore this process in the right way, it would necessarily lead to the discovery of God.

Comment: It would take us beyond dualities. It is like a *koan.*

Dr. Hora: Exactly, it is a *koan. Koan* is a Japanese word meaning "riddle." Life is a riddle, have you ever noticed that? And one of the many riddles of life is the phenomenon of victimization. Has anyone here ever been a victim?

Comment: Yes.

Comment: But you say there are no victims.

Dr. Hora: I didn't say that. I said there are no involuntary victims.

Some time in the not too distant future it may be discovered that it is hopeless to ask the six futile questions. It will be discovered that in all these thousands of years answers could not be found because the questions asked were invalid. And as long as we ask invalid questions, we will never find valid answers. We must ask the right questions and then we will find valid answers and solutions to problems. It is possible that victimology will hasten the discovery of the importance of asking the right questions, because it is so urgent and pressing and universally afflictive. It is very frustrating that no answers are being found; we can find viruses that seemingly cause colds, and we can find all sorts of chemical compounds on which certain diseases can be blamed. Crime is also being blamed nowadays on eating the wrong foods. But we cannot find a virus which could cause people to be victims of crime.

Question: Is there really something called victimology? Or did you just make it up?

Dr. Hora: Yes, there is, but not many people know about it.

Comment: The premise of victimology is necessarily on a somewhat higher level than other "ologies."

Dr. Hora: What could be beyond victimology? "Freedomology." In what way can freedom be found in the midst of an epidemic of crime? In what way can man find peace, assurance, freedom, gratitude, love, life in the midst of an epidemic of crime? Wherein lies safety? Safety lies in understanding that the solution to the problem is not in society, in the police, or in the women's liberation movement, but in consciousness. A certain quality of consciousness will create a predilection to victimization, and another quality of consciousness will create a sense of safety.

Comment: I think it is good to include consideration of the criminal too, not only of the victim.

Dr. Hora: Victim and victimizer are both involved in a mental preoccupation with which the culture, at this time, seems to be saturated. Liberation, protection, safety, and peace can be found in attaining a quality of consciousness which the Bible describes as: ". . . dwelling in the secret place of the most High, under the shadow of the Almighty" (Psalm 91). Now isn't this just foolish religious mumbo jumbo? Can the secret place of the most High give us a sense of protection and safety? Actual safety?

Comment: I have seen that as long as I am concerned about

self, everything is self-confirmation, whether it is rape or colds or whatever. And as soon as I turn my attention, my complete attention, to what really is, it disappears and there is peace.

Dr. Hora: The Bible further says in Psalm 91, "Because thou hast made the Lord which is my refuge, even the most High, thy habitation, there shall no evil befall thee, neither shall any [rapist] come nigh thy dwelling." Then the liberation from the fear of crime and rape is to be found in taking refuge in the secret place of the most High, and establishing our dwelling place in the consciousness of divine reality. Is this really possible?

Comment: I think the original question was whether it is possible not to have a bad reaction to such a report.

Dr. Hora: The issue is not how to react, the issue is how to be safe. If we want to be safe, we have to learn how to dwell in the secret place of the most High all the time, how to make the Lord our refuge and our dwelling place.

Comment: Jesus said: "The prince of this world cometh, and hath nothing in me" (John 14:30). Which means that he simply didn't cherish any of the ideas which saturated the culture.

Dr. Hora: In other words, only three things can hurt us: what we cherish, what we hate, and what we fear. Now what happens to these three mental preoccupations when we succeed in making God our dwelling place?

Comment: They disappear from thought.

Dr. Hora: That's right. We cannot serve two masters at the same time. We cannot think two thoughts at the same time. In other words, there must be a shift in priorities and the ego must be allowed to die. Can you see that victimology, of necessity, will have to lead to the discovery of God as a practical reality?

Comment: I would like to see that, but when will that happen?

Comment: Unfortunately, it must happen on an individual basis, but in the future more and more people may become receptive to this and will discover the futility of asking the wrong questions.

Dr. Hora: Pretty soon, we hope, it will become common knowledge that the remedy to crime is in consciousness and not in the police department or the welfare department, not even in the school system or academic education, but in learning how to dwell in the consciousness of divine reality, and in learning how not to be impressed by the fashionable preoccupations of the culture. Would it be helpful for us to avoid television, newspapers, radio?

Comment: Not necessarily. Jesus was not avoiding the evils of his day.

Dr. Hora: In other words, ignorance is not bliss. How do we deal with the aggressive suggestions of the culture which are constantly flooding our consciousness with trash?

Question: Is confronting our fears better?

Dr. Hora: Certainly we must develop an awareness of what we are thinking at all times, and then we can quietly reject and eject whatever garbage thoughts are circulating in our consciousness. It is like wanting to live in a clean apartment; the moment some dirt comes in, the best thing is to sweep it out right away, not let it stand till Wednesday or when the maid comes. Right away, whenever some impurity enters our dwelling place, we quickly remove it, we don't let it stay there.

Comment: Perhaps what is needed is to develop a strong spiritual identity.

Dr. Hora: What is a strong spiritual identity? It is in proportion to our love of purity, order, harmony, peace, assurance, gratitude. The more we appreciate these qualities of consciousness, the stronger we become spiritually, and then we shall not be tempted to allow garbage thoughts to fester in our consciousness. No matter how much garbage there will be around us, in our dwelling place there be purity.

The next question is: "What is a compassionate and comforting way to talk to a friend who has been through such an experience?" Can we go over to her and say: "Ha, ha! You brought it on yourself by not wanting to be raped. Would that be comforting?"

Comment: It could be that the best thing would be to say, "I am sorry," and that's all.

Dr. Hora: That's all?

Comment: The most helpful thing is to know that the individual is a spiritual being, a child of God.

Dr. Hora: Jesus was also called the Comforter. What made him the Comforter? Was he a nice person, did he use pretty words? He would have known that nothing could really happen to a person who was physically violated. If we would meet our friend, and if we really understood that the true individuality of our friend is intact because it cannot be touched physically, if we really knew this in the secret recesses of our mind, what would happen?

Comment: The memory of her experience would be erased.

Dr. Hora: It would disappear from her memory bank, and it would be as if she had seen it in a dream or in the movies, but had not been touched by that experience. In other words, the aftereffects of that experience would be instantaneously erased and healed. And that would be rather comforting, wouldn't it? What we know can be very comforting. What we say is often irrelevant. Either it does nothing or it may make things worse. On a tape recorder, when we record a new message over an old one, what happens to the old one? It gets erased, right? Now when a comforter gets in touch with a comfortee, a new message is being recorded in the consciousness of the so-called victim, and the memory of that experience is erased. And that's very comforting.

Question: Does it depend on the receptivity of the comfortee? Do some people enjoy too much the memory of their victimization?

Dr. Hora: Yes, there is that element in it. Not even Jesus could comfort everybody; there were skeptics and hardened sinners and Pharisees. Referring to them, he said: "Don't throw your pearls before swine," or "Don't give that which is sacred unto dogs." He meant unreceptive thought.

Dialogue No. 18.

PROTECTION

Question: I wanted to ask you about "letting be." I think you have defined it as "reverent, loving, choiceless awareness of what is." It seems to me that sometimes letting someone be doesn't work.

Dr. Hora: Could you give us an example of what you mean?

Comment: Let's take, for instance, a teen-ager. I have this teen-ager at home, and if I let her be, then, according to you, I would expect to see a spiritual child of God emerging, isn't that so? But what I do see is someone who is addicted to television. Now, do I let her be? What does "letting be" mean in this case?

Dr. Hora: Before answering this question, let us analyze it. You are really asking: "What should I do so that my daughter should not watch so much television?" And as you well know, this is one of the dumb questions which unenlightened people are inclined to ask.

Now let us consider the problem. You have a teenage daughter at home who is watching too much television. Wishing to stop your daughter from watching television, you ask us how the concept of "letting be" might be applied to this end.

Question: Do we have to find out what the meaning of this girl's television watching is?

Dr. Hora: No. It would be wiser to start out with seeking to understand the meaning of her mother's concern.

Comment: There seems to be a fear that the child may be susceptible to influences coming from the television programs.

Dr. Hora: Yes. This is a correct perception of the concern. It is a fear that the daughter might be wrongly influenced by some of the inane programs on television, and that false values will be instilled in her. This seems to be a legitimate concern about the values the child is being exposed to. Now the question is, what relevancy does "letting be" have in facing such a problem?

Comment: It seems to me that the only time I have learned something of the truth was in the context of "shouldlessness," and it always came to me as a discovery.

Dr. Hora: What you are really implying here is a procedure which a parent could follow. By becoming "shouldless" she would allow her daughter to come to her senses and stop watching television, or lose interest in watching it. Then, what you are really saying is that the way to get the child to stop watching television is by using "shouldlessness" on her. This sounds good but it is still thinking in terms of means and ends, it is an operational strategy. Hidden in this reasoning there still lurks the futile question: "What to do?" or "How to do it?"

Until now the question was about "letting be" and the answers were about how not to leave alone. To understand the difference between "letting be" and "leaving alone" or "not leaving alone" is very important, and it is subtle, requiring deep understanding. Certainly, "letting be" is the best possible position to take in face of any problem or concern, fear or emotional involvement. What does it mean to "let be" and how can it be helpful?

Comment: That's the big question.

Dr. Hora: Let us consider the principle of harmonious living. In what way could that help us in this situation? The principle of harmonious living says: "Take no thought for what should be or shouldn't be; seek ye first to know the good of God which already is."

Comment: This principle alters our horizontal, "self-and-other" thinking, and lifts our consciousness to an awareness of God's power and presence.

Dr. Hora: Suppose you were a mother and you were confronted with a concern like the one just discussed. You know about "letting be," and you know about the principle of harmonious living, and you have attained "shouldlessness." How would you then protect your child? Is protection possible?

Comment: I would get her interested in something else permanently, then she would forget about watching television.

Dr. Hora: Now what kind of reasoning is this again?

Comment: It is still operational reasoning.

Question: Even if I could get her interested in spiritual values?

Dr. Hora: Spiritual values are not a means to an end, they are the end.

Comment: Perhaps what is needed is more than "letting be," namely, letting God be. Because everything else is just a disguised form of manipulative thinking.

Dr. Hora: This is excellent. Of course letting God be God is the supreme prayer, and when we let God be God, we are totally "shouldless" and non-operational, non-meddling. We are fearless and there is a climate of trust within us and around us. Jesus said: "Behold, I give you power to tread on serpents and scorpions, and over all the power of the enemy [which includes television]: and nothing shall by any means hurt you" (Luke 10:19). What is this power which Jesus refers to? This power lies in radical reliance on God.

Question: What about spiritual progress, isn't it a "should"? Can we make spiritual progress without "should-ing" ourselves to make this progress?

Dr. Hora: This is an interesting question. What happens to us when we become willful about studying spiritual truths? You understand that "should" indicates a willfulness in our approach. We become self-righteous or very frustrated, and we may wind up shaking our fist at heaven and getting into conflict with God. It is not advisable to approach anything in life in a willful way. There is a story about a man who ordered a motorcycle from Japan. When he opened the package, he found the instruction sheet, which read: "Before assembling motorcycle, obtain peace of mind." We cannot take the kingdom of God by storm. We must seek and knock and ask devotedly with reverent, loving receptivity.

Dialogue No. 19

SUBSTANCE

Question: If things go well, we don't take credit for it, we are just grateful to God. How are we to think about the situations where things are going wrong? How can we not blame ourselves?

Dr. Hora: Well, what is the difference between blame and credit?

Comment: No difference.

Dr. Hora: So if we cannot take credit for the good, we cannot take blame for the bad. Isn't that wonderful?

Question: How are we to understand experiences which are inharmonious, discordant, troublesome?

Comment: For many years things were not going well in my life, and yet they were always going well; I just had the impression that they weren't going well. All that was needed was for me to be able to see that everything was already perfect. And so it isn't really true that things are not going well.

Question: Is the problem then that we think things should go in a certain way?

Dr. Hora: That is certainly part of it. There is a universal desire to take credit and to take blame. What is the meaning of that desire?

Comment: We find those things self-confirmatory.

Dr. Hora: If we cannot take credit and if we cannot take blame, what can we take? Where does it leave us? It leaves us with the questions: "Who are we? What are we?" Is there something relevant to this question in the Bible? St. Paul said: "If a man think himself to be something, when he is nothing, he deceiveth himself" (Galatians 6:3). Where does that leave us? Are we nothing? Man is a very strange creature. Some people believe that belittling themselves and blaming themselves is a sign of humility. In certain circles it is fashionable to blame oneself. This is masquerading as humility, but it isn't; it is just a reverse form of boasting. We cannot boast—that's obvious—but neither can we not boast. What can we do? This is an invalid question.

Comment: We have to see life from a spiritual perspective.

Dr. Hora: Yes. Now what happens when we see life from a spiritual perspective, when there is neither boasting nor not boasting?

Comment: We are not concerned with the self at all. We realize that we are reflections of God and we manifest that.

Dr. Hora: Right. What are we concerned with if we are not concerned with the self? So we do not keep asking who is to blame, who is to get credit. What are we asking?

Comment: What is what really *is?*

Dr. Hora: Yes, and then everything is clear, good, very simple, and all problems are solved because God has already made it good. Sometimes people think that there are too many restrictions on our conversation; we cannot say this and we cannot say that; we cannot ask this and we cannot ask that; we cannot boast and we cannot feel guilty. There does not seem anything left. And it would seem that all these restrictions are taking all the fun out of life. What are we doing? We are peeling an onion, so to speak, to get to the core. What happens when we peel an onion? What is at the core of an onion?

Comment: Nothing.

Dr. Hora: Exactly. And that is what Saint Paul was talking about. At the core of an onion we discover the Nothing. And that is what really is. So what's so good about nothing?

Comment: That's no-thing, no materiality.

Dr. Hora: Yes. We discover nothingness. Nothingness is not zero, it is what really is. How is that possible? Can that be?

Comment: It seems very strange, but when we try to solve our problems from a material point of view, there is a great deal of suffering. We are told that we can find solutions if we attain the spiritual point of view. And one does not want to pass up this opportunity; if that's true, we want to try it. We want to get to the point where we can find out whether it is really true, because the other way there is not much help. I have in my class at present two children who are undergoing intensive psychiatric therapy. These children are immobilized, and whatever seems to be the problem, it is obviously not helped and the families are suffering.

Dr. Hora: Is it really helpful to realize nothingness? Does it really solve problems? Or are we just kidding ourselves? Is it just wishful thinking?

Comment: No. The other day I had an experience where everything seemed to go awfully wrong. I actually realized that all the conniving, manipulating, and vengeful thinking which was flooding my consciousness would in no way solve my problem. I would be miserable as usual, and the situation wouldn't change. I realized that I could do nothing of my own self, and I found great relief in letting God take care of me. And the next day at work all things were harmonious and peaceful.

Dr. Hora: That sounds like magic, doesn't it?

Comment: I guess what is needed is a complete sense of God and the awareness of spiritual values right where the problem seems to be.

Dr. Hora: Yes, of course. Sometimes we observe such impressive results that it looks like a miracle. But miracles do not exist, they are just things we do not understand. Somebody had a growth on his face and he prayed about it. And he prayed well because, a few days later, he looked in the mirror and the growth was still there, but when he touched it with his finger, it fell off. There was a little bleeding which soon stopped, and there was no trace of it afterwards.

Question: How does one pray well? What does it mean to pray well?

Comment: I think it means to pray sincerely.

Dr. Hora: Yes, sincerely, but with understanding. In order to understand such "miracles," we have to understand the reality of nothingness and the unreality of somethingness. How can we say such a thing? Isn't that absurd? We can put it this way: We have to understand the substantiality of nothingness and the insubstantiality of somethingness.

Comment: Maybe it would help to know that the growth on his face was thought, and that thought is nothing.

Dr. Hora: Personhood is just an idea. If people have personal problems, then they have invented them.

Comment: This reminds me of what happened to me with my facial twitch. I had a twitch for about ten years around my eye, and doctors told me there was nothing they could do. I consulted all kinds of doctors. And when Dr. Hora told me that this was only a thought, I didn't believe him. But it was revealed to me that it was the expression of my fear of facing my thoughts about my daughter. And I don't know exactly when it happened, but the twitch is gone.

Dr. Hora: Thoughts come and thoughts go. When we see something tangible and visible, we assume that it is real. If we can touch it, feel it, measure it, cut it with a knife, we believe it must be real. But actually it isn't. If we substitute the word "substance" for "real," then it will become clearer. What seems to be substantial to us is really nothing but thought in visible form. The man with the growth, for example. He could touch the growth, he could pull on it, it was bleeding, and it was growing, but it was just a thought, it wasn't really substantial.

Question: Is this how he prayed, recognizing in prayer that it was not substantial?

Dr. Hora: Yes, something to that effect. He tried to understand that he is made of spirit, that his substance is spiritual, and that he is perfect even as God his creator is perfect. Once we come even to suspect that the tangible is not substantial and the intangible is substantial, then we are already beginning to understand something that can heal any problem. One of you told us about your healing after you realized that personality frictions on the job were not realities, but merely thoughts making themselves felt as realities. You gained a sense of peace in the knowledge of the truth that in divine reality these things do not exist because they are just inventions of human imagination.

The moment we catch a glimpse of the fact that what seems to be tangible, what we can suffer from, is insubstantial, and that perfect harmony and spiritual life is the real life, then we have destroyed the problem. Where have we destroyed the problem? In our thoughts. In our consciousness. We have destroyed the problem and it is gone. If the basis of all problems is thought, then we can destroy any problem in consciousness. Some people might say: Well, that's just wishful thinking, magical thinking, fancy, or fantasy. It would be so if it were not based on a solid understanding of what God is, of what divine reality is. If it is based on a solid understanding of what divine reality is, the validity of our proposition proves itself in the disappearance of the problem. Be it personal, financial, occupational, or physical.

Comment: There was a time when I was working for the American Cancer Society, and all the propaganda was filling my consciousness. I thought then that cancer was something to be feared. We had a poodle at that time who had to be taken to the vet. He found some disorder and sent us to a specialist. This man was a nationally known cancer specialist. He said the dog had a malignant tumor and had to be operated on. I called Dr. Hora because I was so upset that I couldn't even think. At that time I understood very little about spiritual reality. Dr. Hora calmed my thoughts. Next day, I took the dog to the hospital to be operated on. They prepared the dog for the operation and examined him internally and found no trace of a disease. The tumor had disappeared and there was no trace of it. The surgeon was very embarrassed in front of his colleagues because he had diagnosed it, located it, and now he had to admit that it just wasn't there. He told me to take the dog home because there was nothing wrong with him. At that time, I had no understanding of the disappearance of what seemed to be so real. Later, however, I was able to understand and to know what really happened. This experience taught me much and it was very helpful to me later on.

Dr. Hora: The important thing is to reach a point where it is clear to us that the tangible is insubstantial and the intangible is substantial. Spirit is the substance of everything that really is; and whatever seems to be—whether it is steel or gold or diamond, or flesh or blood—is not really substance. It is rather difficult to comprehend that.

Let us consider the question of context. We speak about living in the context of divine reality. What do we mean by that?

Comment: Framework, perspective, background.

Dr. Hora: These are synonyms. Isn't everyone seeing life in that context? In what context do unenlightened people live their lives?

Comment: In the context of self, ego, sensation, emotion, material possession.

Dr. Hora: What is the most frequent context in which sophisticated people live nowadays?

Comment: Interpersonal relationships.

Dr. Hora: Context is that which is uppermost in our thinking, and psychologically sophisticated people see life in a horizontal context of a relationship of self and others. This context is, of course, unreal and full of trouble. It is thinking about what others are thinking about what we are thinking. What happens when we emigrate from that world and take up citizenship in the kingdom of God? What happens to our outlook when we take up residence in the kingdom of God?

Comment: Everything you see is expressing God and it is good. Our orientation is toward the good. Instead of having a taste of stirring up strife, we would become interested in harmony, the beautiful and the good, the true, in being beneficial. It is an entirely different life.

Dr. Hora: In the context of divine reality, whatever is important to other people is unimportant to us; and everything that is important to us is important to the whole world. How is that?

Comment: Because that's real and that's what everybody really wants, although they may not know it.

Dr. Hora: That's right. And so it happens that we become beneficial presences in the world.

Dialogue No. 20

PARASITISM

Question: What is the meaning of parasitic infestation?

Dr. Hora: Parasites in our lives and experiences indicate the presence of parasitic thinking in our consciousness. It is necessary to be willing to be embarrassed if we want to understand the meaning of our problems. It is embarrassing to discover parasitic thinking in ourselves. *Nihil humanum me alienum puto,* which means, nothing human is alien to me.

As long as we consider ourselves human beings, we have to believe that nothing human is alien to us, that we are capable of any depredations. But are we human? What is a human being? According to Freud, a human being is a civilized savage, a polymorphous perverse individual. What did he mean? He had a rather bad opinion about people. Polymorphous perverse means capable of any kind of perversity or bestiality. Therefore, as long as we believe that we are human, we can console ourselves by saying: "After all, I am only human." But the Bible says that we are not human, that we are spiritual manifestations of God, incapable of anything evil. "Thou art of purer eyes than to behold evil, and canst not look on iniquity" (Habakkuk 1:13).

In the human condition, parasitism and envy are but minor vices. Parasitism means to exploit, to use, and to want to get something for nothing, mostly from other people. Parasitic thinking is very common, and is practically universal in children. After all, up to a certain age, children are parasites, literally sucking nourishment out of their mothers.

There is an infinite variety of possibilities of parasitic thinking. It is good to reach a point of willingness to be embarrassed about ourselves and say: "This is no good. This is human, and nothing human can ever be valid or healthy or wholesome. We must reject it radically, categorically, and absolutely." We must say: "I am not a human parasite. I am a spiritual manifestation of Love-Intelligence, an emanation of God, God's grace is my sufficiency in all things. Everything I need comes from God." Is that possible? Can money come from God? Can emotional gratification come from God? Can happiness come from God? Can self-esteem come from God? Can job security come from God? How can all these things we need come from a source that is invisible and whose reality is in dispute?

It is interesting that parasitism is a prolific source of poverty —financial, emotional, and any other kind of poverty. It is based on the fantasy that somebody else has and "I don't have, therefore, I need." And it is this thinking that keeps an individual in poverty. What is the secret formula for wealth and riches which is described in the Bible and which was annunciated by Jesus? What is this formula for being wealthy? "For whosoever hath, to him shall be given and he shall have more abundance; but whosoever hath not, from him shall be taken away even that he hath" (Matthew 13:12). Is that fair? This saying is very interesting, because if we look at it from a human standpoint, it is utterly unfair and completely irrational. But Jesus never spoke from a human perspective. He was speaking from a divine perspective and he was annunciating a divine principle.

A parasitically inclined individual always thinks of himself as a have-not; he always thinks that others have and he does not have. This is his essential outlook on life. Mentally he has labeled himself as a have-not, and he lives in the future, thinking that one of these days he is going to get from somebody who has. Now, "as he thinketh in his heart, so is he" (Proverbs 23:7), and the future will never come because in the future he will still be thinking that he does not have. We can only be wealthy if we are convinced that we have. How can we be convinced that we have if our pockets are empty? Or if we are out of a job? Again, our dilemma is that we keep slipping into human reasoning and seeing ourselves as human. But if we are alert and refuse the temptation of interpreting this magnificent principle within the human context, and if we stay with the spiritual perspective, then we see that there is no individual who would not have an infinite supply of intelligence, of love, of goodwill, of gratitude, of joy, of spiritual riches. Therefore, it is possible for everybody to start thinking of himself as having, as "one who hath."

Once we begin to see that we really have everything that is really precious in life, we have it. And pretty soon we will find that more is given to us, more and more is just coming in. When someone starts telling me, "Oh, we are short of money, business is not good," I say, "Stop, you are hurting yourself." It is dangerous to think that we lack something, because the moment we think that way, we will experience it. In divine reality there is no such thing as lack of anything, and an enlightened man is always seeing himself and others in the context of divine reality.

What does it mean to be irrational? It is impossible to be irrational; it is only possible to live in another dimension or context. In the human dimension of reasoning, what Jesus said does not make any sense at all; it is irrational. But if we live in the dimension of divine reality, everything that Jesus said is very rational, intelligent, beautiful, helpful, and good.

Of course, there seem to be crazy people who speak spiritual lingo and quote the Bible. These are the religiously insane. How can we tell whether someone is enlightened or just an instance of pathological religiosity? There are two things we must watch out for: first of all, the sick man is exploiting whatever he knows in order to confirm himself; he is promoting himself subtly or brazenly; he is bragging. Secondly, he wants to influence people. These two signs indicate that something is wrong. When someone really understands, he is considerate, humble, modest, and unobtrusive. He is not advocating what he believes in, nor is he promoting himself.

What did Jesus have to say about such people? "Beware of false prophets, which come to you in sheep's clothing, but inwardly they are ravening wolves. Ye shall know them by their fruits" (Matthew 7:15,16). Jesus covered all possible contingencies. There is no problem in life that we could not find answers to in searching his teachings. What did he say about people who are religious and hope for a reward? There are people who pray to God to get something. This is parasitism introduced into religion; one can carry parasitism into one's relationship to God. How naïve this is! Can one con God? Jesus said: "But when ye pray, use not vain repetitions as the heathen do: for they think that they shall be heard for their much speaking" (Matthew 6:7).

Parasitism does not work on the human level and it does not work in our relationship to God. We don't have to ask anything of God because we have already been given everything good.

Parasitism can take the form of homosexuality, heterosexuality, or marriage, which is conceived of as an interpersonal relationship. The idea is to get something from each other, such as love, affection, compliments, and particularly sexual power. In homosexuality we see that participants in the homosexual relationships frequently have a belief that the other fellow has great sexual power, and his partner has a great need of sexual power. So they enter into partnership—male or female. It is all based on the idea that one has what the other needs, and that they give it to one another in the sexual act. This is a fantasy. There are many other possibilities of fantasies, such as sadomasochistic fantasies, where one has a desire to hurt and the other has the wish to be hurt, and so they feed on one another in fantasy. This can happen in heterosexual relationships as well. The basic idea is always that one can get something vitally important from another person.

If we have a horizontal perspective on reality, we try to get everything we believe we have need for from each other. And that is called human relationship. Of course, this is full of problems. But when we come to see through the eyes of Jesus, which is divine reality, then our horizontal, flat outlook on life becomes full-dimensional and we discover that we do not have to use people to get what we think we need, that we already have everything we need. The sun is already shining

on the black and the white and the green. We are joint participants in the good of God, and we see ourselves as infinitely
rich and blessed and endowed with an abundance of everything good.

Does enlightened man seek emotional gratification? Only
human beings desire emotional gratification. There are people who love to go to funerals. They go to funerals to have
an emotional release by immersing themselves in the conta-
gion of crying. At a funeral, crying is socially acceptable, and
some people love to cry. Of course, there are other forms of
emotional gratification, like hating, cursing, spitting, or whatever.

In the realm of divine reality there is no need for emotional
outlet. What happens to the emotions when man becomes
enlightened? "All things work together for good" (Romans
8:28). There is no problem. There is no need for special
attention to affective control. It is interesting that in the Bible
there are four scenes where Jesus seemed to have behaved
like a human being, and many theologians and preachers are
inclined to make a big issue out of it. Once, in the synagogue,
where he seemed to have been angry, even belligerent. It is
claimed that he had an emotional reaction. Another was at the
tomb of Lazarus, where he supposedly cried. Third was on the
cross, where he supposedly complained. People seize on that
and hope to discredit everything he said. It probably wasn't
true at all. These things are not part and parcel of his teachings. They do not fit the total picture. It must have been an
interpretation of what people thought he was doing. He did
not say he was angry, he just said: "Make not my Father's
house an house of merchandise" (John 2:16). And whether he
cried at the tomb of Lazarus, how can we know? Another
place where he was supposed to have cried was in the garden
of Gethsemane. Nobody saw that he was sweating blood because his friends were sleeping. It must be a writer's fantasy.
He was too advanced for such human frailties. It does not
make any sense and it is unimportant anyway. But people tend
to pick it up and make a big issue out of it. Some would like
to drag him down into the human dimension; others want to

deify him. But he was neither human nor God. He was just at an advanced state of spiritual consciousness. Being God is not real for man, being human is also not real. But being a spiritual consciousness—that's real. And that's what he was.

Dialogue No. 21

SELF-PITY

Comment: Recently I was given an assignment from school to write an autobiography. I approached it with great hesitation, and I found it hard to do. After I was finished with it, I discovered that it was full of self-pity and complaints.

Dr. Hora: This is a very important discovery. The Bible says: "As man thinketh in his heart, so is he" (Proverbs 23:7). And we could add, and so will his life be also. Nothing comes into experience uninvited. We think in secret and it comes to pass; the world is but our looking glass. If we are in the habit of complaining and feeling sorry for ourselves, believing that we are unfairly treated, then our entire destiny will be shaped accordingly. We are inviting maltreatment. There are no involuntary victims, no persecutions come our way uninvited. Does it mean that we are to blame for our misfortune? Does it mean we are to blame for being poor? It is very important to know not to ask futile questions—especially "Who is to blame?"—when someone is inviting a miserable life for himself.

Comment: Ignorance is to blame.

Dr. Hora: Right. What evidence is there that this is so?

Comment: When ignorance disappears, healing occurs.

Dr. Hora: When ignorance disappears, healing does not occur. When does healing occur? When the truth appears in consciousness. Suppose we discover that two and two is not five; does it mean that we already know arithmetic? What evidence do we have that no one is to blame, only ignorance? What is the difference between truths and facts?

Comment: Facts are appearances.

Dr. Hora: That's right. And what is truth?

Comment: Truth is what is real.

Dr. Hora: That's right. If we ask wrong questions about

self-pity—such as, "Why do I have this problem?" "Who is to blame for it?" "What should I do about it?" "How should I do it?" —we will never find a solution. But if we ask "What is the meaning of self-pity?" then the answer is "It is a self-confirmatory idea."

Question: So what?

Dr. Hora: Now we know the meaning of self-pity, and now we can ask the second intelligent question: "What is what really *is*?" You realized that writing a self-confirmatory autobiography is not what really *is*, it is not the truth of your being, so you changed it. What really *is*, is the good of God—perfect being.

However, there is usually a certain reluctance to part with self-pity. What is the meaning of that reluctance? We enjoy self-confirmatory ideation, it is a form of self-indulgence. If we have an itch, it is pleasurable to scratch it. All human problems originate in self-confirmatory thinking. Once we understand that, we shall guard ourselves against this tendency as against the plague. The remedy to every problem is to come to know who we really are and what is what really *is*.

Question: I have a problem with skepticism. I find it difficult to pray because I doubt whether there really is a God, or anything. How does one overcome skepticism?

Dr. Hora: Little by little. Today someone told me a story about opening the Bible at random in the morning and finding a passage in the Book of Ezekiel which said: "Thou art a whore for thou hast many lovers besides thine husband." This individual thought to herself: "This is ridiculous, I am not even married." So she closed the Bible and put it aside. While on the bus traveling to work, she pulled out a small Bible which she carries in her purse and opened it at random —as is her habit to do—and her eyes fell on the following quotation: "Thou art a whore for thou hast many lovers besides thine husband." This time she took notice of it, and it occurred to her that the Bible also says: "Thy Maker is thine husband" (Isaiah: 54:5). Suddenly, everything became clear to her, and she knew that this message was from God specifically addressed to her to meet her need for spiritual commitment.

Such little experiences are not uncommon with sincere students of the way, and they help us to see the validity of everything that we are learning about God as divine Principle and Cosmic Consciousness. Nothing happens by chance, everything is a continuous unfolding of the activity of divine Mind.

Dialogue No. 22

PLEASURE AND JOY

Question: Some people are under treatment for various reasons by a number of doctors at the same time. What could be the meaning of that?

Dr. Hora: Some people enjoy having things done to them, they like to be objects of manipulation. They like to be targets of positive or negative attention. It is a way of using other people to confirm oneself as a physical personality. As long as there is such a desire, there is no possibility of being healthy because the body is forever asking for some kind of attention. What does the Bible say about that? "The flesh lusteth against the Spirit" (Galatians 5:17). What does "lusteth" mean? It means strong pleasurable desire. By lusting for pleasurable physical excitement we are lusting against spiritual liberation.

Comment: It is an amazingly efficient statement; if we tried to say it any other way, it would take a couple of sentences.

Dr. Hora: It is very effective communication. What are fantasies? They are more or less disguised ways of lusting or craving physical experiences, either pleasurable or painful, and thereby removing ourselves from spiritual realization. What would life be like without fantasies and daydreams? Would it not be very empty and boring to live without daydreams? What would life be like without television?

Question: The internal or the external?

Dr. Hora: There is a meaningful parallel between the television in the living room and the one in consciousness. Long before television for the living room was invented, there was "television" in consciousness. The television is just an external appearance of what already existed in consciousness long ago.

There is a German painter by the name of Balthus who

portrays people as daydreamers. The most important aspect of his work is that everyone he portrays is a sleepwalker and a masturbator, children and adults alike. He portrays the human condition as people living in their fantasies even while they are pursuing their daily activities. I think he tried to wake up the world by his work, because the way to wake up is to become aware that we are asleep.

Question: Wouldn't it be more helpful to portray a man who is awake?

Dr. Hora: How would you portray a man who is awake?

Comment: I am thinking of the statue of the Buddha which we discussed previously, which portrays such qualities as peace, joy, compassion.

Dr. Hora: What is required for permanent wakefulness? It requires a willingness to reject pleasure. Would you be willing to reject pleasure?

Comment: Only if I really knew that something better is available.

Dr. Hora: In what way is the willingness to reject pleasure going to help us to wake up? We are all quite willing to reject pain and fear, but unless we are willing to reject pleasure, there is no possibility of awakening, because the moment we accept pleasure, we also accept pain and fear. It is not possible to reject pain without rejecting pleasure because they are inseparable, they are two sides of the same coin.

What does it mean to reject pleasure? We know what it means to reject pain. If we reach the point of not desiring pleasure, we have it made. To reject pleasure does not mean to impose a painful way of life upon ourselves. To reject pleasure means to lose interest in every thought which has the promise of some kind of pleasurable outcome.

Question: What happens to sex then?

Comment: A few months ago, I read in a book that one must give up pleasure just for the sake of pleasure. And I began to understand how one can eat not for pleasure but for nourishment.

Dr. Hora: That is very interesting. Could you explain how this principle relates to sex?

Comment: If sex is approached in pursuit of pleasurable sensations alone, then there is no love. If there is love to begin with, then sex isn't even thought of as sex but is part of a whole harmonious expression.

Dr. Hora: The rejection of pleasure is the rejection of the pursuit of pleasure. Nothing must be done in the pursuit of pleasure. We can eat with pleasure, but we must never eat for pleasure. Usually, however, we get so hooked on pleasure that all our motives and actions are completely perverted. We don't go to a restaurant anymore to eat, we go there for entertainment. An automobile may not be a conveyance, it may turn into an instrument of pleasure. Sex has become a form of entertainment, and most everything is perverted into the pursuit of pleasure. Naturally, if our thought processes are oriented toward pleasure, we are in for a lot of pain and fear.

When we wake up, we discover joy and we lose interest in pleasure per se. And then we can throw the television set out of our consciousness. Our motivations become more wholesome. The Zen Master says: "When I am hungry, I eat, when I am tired, I rest." It is hard to give up daydreams and fantasies as long as we believe that pleasure is important, and so we cannot wake up and we cannot shake off the fantasies.

We need to cultivate an appreciation of joy. Then our fantasies will leave us, and with it illnesses and problems. Every illness, whether it is physical, psychological, emotional, or economic, is just the expression of certain fantasies entertained in the pursuit of pleasure. For instance, a man may have a fantasy that on his job he is getting a great deal of pleasure for being important, and other employees are afraid of him. He has a fantasy of being powerful and important. This fantasy gives him a great deal of pleasure and he is hooked on it. As a result of this fantasy—which can be conscious or unconscious—he becomes an insufferable bore and gets kicked out. Then he has pain; the pleasure turned into pain, and the whole thing is just a dream, which is like a sickness.

When we believe that the important thing in life is to have

pleasure, we start producing fantasies leading to that pleasure, and organizing our mode of being-in-the-world in such a way as to enjoy this pleasure. Then, of course, this pleasure makes us an unbeneficial presence in the world and we suffer the consequences. It is therefore important to wake up.

There is no such thing as a need for pleasure; pleasure is always something we want. It is a distortion of the concept of good. There is a need to be joyous. It is an existential requirement to be joyous. No one has a need for pleasure.

Dialogue No. 23

FRICTIONLESSNESS

Question: Dr. Hora, you occasionally refer to God as consciousness. Could you please explain the meaning of that term?

Dr. Hora: What mystifies you about that word?

Comment: I always thought of it more in connection with man, sort of that it is up to us to be conscious of God.

Question: When we ascribe awareness to God, isn't it anthropomorphic?

Dr. Hora: Let us consider the meaning of the word "anthropomorphic."

Comment: Thinking of God as manlike.

Dr. Hora: Anthropomorphic means having the appearance of man. *Morphos, morphein,* means form; anthropomorphic means in the form of man (*anthropos* = man). Anthropomorphic God means in the form of man. But when we speak of consciousness, we are not anthropomorphizing God. What are we doing? We are making man Godlike. God is not manlike, man is Godlike. How is that possible?

In order for God to be manlike, God would have to have a form, and that is impossible because form is finite. God is infinite, indefinite, undefined. Therefore, if man is Godlike, we are saying that man has something in common with God. We do not have our physical bodies in common with God. God doesn't have a physical body. So how can we say that man is Godlike? There must be something that we have in common with God. It is consciousness, the faculty to be aware of the thoughts passing through and being present in consciousness—this is the quality we have in common with God. God is Cosmic Consciousness and man is the individualized reflection, manifestation, representation, and misrepresentation of this divine consciousness.

Now what is the shape of consciousness? Consciousness has no shape. It is undefined, indefinite, infinite. So man is infinite consciousness within the infinite consciousness which is God. *Omnis in omnis.*

Question: When we speak of levels of consciousness, isn't it one of those misrepresentations which you alluded to?

Dr. Hora: Misrepresentations are sometimes helpful.

Comment: It has something to do with the quality of perception.

Dr. Hora: Right. The higher the level of consciousness, the purer and more spiritual is perception, which includes aesthetic appreciation. When we approach enlightenment, our consciousness is elevated to behold spiritual values. Art and beauty are aesthetic values. The higher our level of consciousness, the more we respond to beauty, harmony, truth, joy, freedom, love, integrity. On a lower level of consciousness many of these things escape us.

Comment: This also explains why some people can clearly perceive issues and others not.

Dr. Hora: Recently we spoke about beholding. It is not easy to develop the faculty of beholding. Something has to happen in consciousness in order that this faculty can be awakened within us. Beholding means seeing the invisible, thinking the unthinkable, perceiving the unimaginable, and understanding the inconceivable. Beholding is the secret of effective prayer; otherwise prayer is of little consequence. Jesus said: "God is Spirit, and they that worship him must worship him in spirit and in truth" (John 4:24). When we have learned to behold, we can worship in spirit, and then our prayers become truly effective; otherwise it is mostly an exercise in futility.

Question: How do we work to reach that level?

Dr. Hora: We need some guidance; Jesus said: "I am come a light into the world, that whosoever believeth on me should not abide in darkness" (John 12:46).

An interesting aspect of spiritual life is frictionlessness. The Zen Master Suzuki was asked, "How does it feel to be enlightened?" He answered, "Just like ordinary life, but about two inches above ground." What did he mean? He was alluding to frictionless living. Another Zen saying describes the enlightened man as leaving no footprints behind himself. This is a symbolic way of indicating that in divine reality there is frictionless living. Now we know that if something is frictionless, it will never wear out, it is immortal, eternal.

Consider the pleasures of ordinary living. Everything in unenlightened life is based on friction. Gentle friction is pleasurable, rough friction is pain; but there is always friction, everything involves friction. The basic quality of material life is friction, and unenlightened man is always speculating how to get some pleasurable friction. Sex is friction, violence is friction. Enlightened man is longing to know frictionlessness. Spiritual joy is frictionless happiness.

Since the enlightened man longs for the harmony of frictionless life, he is not easily provoked. The Chinese sage Lao-tse said: "The wise man does not contend, therefore no man can contend against him."

Total frictionlessness is not achieved until ascension. When Jesus ascended, he achieved total frictionlessness. In the Orient this is referred to as Nirvana. But we can greatly improve the quality of our lives and live more harmoniously, peacefully, and effectively, with less wear and tear, if our interest is reoriented away from friction toward the good of God, which is frictionless.

Wouldn't it be nice if there were no need to cope with life? Actually it is possible not to have to cope with life. Coping with life is the result of the erroneous assumption that we have personal power and can, through friction, get what we want. If we understand that we are inseparable from divine consciousness—which is the only power, intelligence, vitality, and good that is really expressing itself in the world—then we can discover a way of life where the issue of coping does not come up. Everything is unfolding according to the best possible way. A higher power and intelligence is in control of everything. When the Zen Master spoke about walking two inches above ground, he also meant to say, "I don't have to cope with life, I am being lived by an infinite intelligence

which is expressing itself through me as infinite good. I don't
have a care in the world, I have no fears or worries of any kind;
there are no obstacles in my path; I don't have to influence
anybody, I don't have to coerce anybody, I don't have to bribe
anybody, I don't have to pressure anybody to get what I want.
Whatever is good and beautiful and intelligent and needful is
unfolding in my life by virtue of my conscious awareness of
what really is."

Jesus said: "In the world ye shall have tribulation: but be
of good cheer; I have overcome the world" (John 16:33).

Question: Is there anything in nature that is frictionless?

Dr. Hora: There is nothing whatsoever in nature that is
frictionless. Even the birds require friction in order to fly.
There is a famous story about Chuang-Tzu, the Chinese
teacher of Taoist wisdom. His disciples came to tell him about
a man who was so enlightened that he could ride on the wind.
But Chuang-Tzu was unimpressed and said: "This man is not
enlightened, he still needs the wind."

Question: What is the meaning of our desire for friction?

Dr. Hora: The pleasure of self-confirmatory awareness. "I
feel, therefore I am."

Question: What is the meaning of dreaming about flying?

Dr. Hora: According to Freud, flying has a sexual meaning.

Comment: According to Freud, everything has a sexual
meaning.

Comment: I used to think of it as having power, as being
above others.

Dr. Hora: Sex can be viewed as having power over others.
Anything can be used as a power manipulation. It is possible
that the desire for sex can hamper us from ascending to a
spiritual plane of consciousness. Certainly, the preoccupation
with sex can be a drag, holding us back from soul-existence.
There are two kinds of existences: sense-existence and soul-
existence. Enlightened life could be called soul-existence; and
ordinary life can be called sense-existence.

Question: Do dreams belong to sense-existence?

Dr. Hora: Yes, as long as the dreamer is unenlightened.

Comment: Lately, I have been indulging myself in eating

chocolates and sweets. Would this hold me back from spiritual progress?

Dr. Hora: Eating sweets would not hold you back, but desiring to eat it would be a hindrance. Sex may not keep you back from spiritual life, but the desire for sex would. What is sense-existence? When we desire pleasure, when we believe that pleasure is the supreme good of life, then we are in sense-existence. When we understand that joy is the good of life, then we enter into soul-existence. So it is not the chocolate that is the problem, nor the sex; the problem is our wrong concept of happiness. In sense-existence we are always looking for friction. The friction of the chocolate flowing down into the stomach, the friction of sexual intercourse, the friction of arguing, or the friction of contending, conflict, violence.

Children and teen-agers are particularly devoted to the pleasures of friction and its pain. In soul-existence we appreciate frictionlessness, joy, harmony, beauty, perfect life without wear and tear, conflict-free; in sense-existence this appears to be very boring and undesirable. But when we discover that this is really very good, and the only good, then we lose interest in sense-existence and in friction.

Progress on the spiritual path is movement from sense to soul. From friction to frictionlessness. From pleasure and pain to pure joy. Now the question is: "Was Freud right about interpreting dreams of flying as sexual in nature?"

Comment: He was sort of half-right, wasn't he? He saw the meaning but he didn't know what really *is.*

Dr. Hora: He was not half-right but completely wrong. His error was based on his belief that the supreme good of life is sexual pleasure, and since flying is pleasurable, he assumed that flying must mean sexual pleasure. He reasoned in this manner without realizing that there is a universal yearning in man for transcendence, or soul-existence. So, quite to the contrary, dreams of flying indicate a longing for that form of happiness which sex can never give, namely, frictionless happiness.

When we are beginning to reach out for soul-existence, we

become aware of how much we are attached to the pleasures of friction, and there is the battle of the flesh against the spirit, and vice versa, until such time that the spirit wins. When frictionless joy, peace, assurance, gratitude, love, and harmony are truly appreciated, then it is easy to turn our attention away from all other forms of pleasure seeking. We give up everything and we discover that we haven't lost anything because we gain the pearl of great price—true happiness.

Question: Does orgasm have a spiritual equivalent? Or what is it? What is orgasm? What is its meaning?

Dr. Hora: Orgasm is a sensory and emotional experience within the context of sexual intercourse or masturbation, and it is always accompanied by fantasies. Jesus said: "In the resurrection they neither marry, nor are given in marriage, but are as the angels of God in heaven" (Matthew 22:30). In the light of Zen Buddhism this saying would probably go as follows: "Enlightened people neither marry nor not marry." What does that mean? It means that enlightened people are not interested in sensual pleasure and fantasies. Just as enlightened people do not eat for pleasure but for nourishment; enlightened people are not pleasure seekers. They are interested in expressing love in every possible way, which may include even sexual intercourse. But the aim is not orgastic pleasure, the aim is the expression of love. There is a difference.

In the modern world after Freud there was an epidemic of pleasure seeking; pleasure was considered the most important pursuit of life. Everything we do must be done in order that pleasure should result. Sex has become entertainment and the orgasm has become the *summum bonum vitae.*

It is not possible to attain orgasm without a friction of some sort. Where there is friction, there is wear and tear. In soul-existence there is no friction, therefore there is no wear and tear, there is no conflict. There is just harmony, peace, assurance, gratitude, love, joy, and immortality. You never get too old or worn out to have joy. Joy is a constant, eternal, immortal condition basic to reality. So the spiritual counterpart of orgasm is joy.

It is important to emphasize that the issue is not abstinence but a realization that it is possible to attain a higher level of consciousness where orgasm has no significance because there is something much better. Unenlightened life is mostly a search for pleasure and entertainment. But this kind of orientation is very troublesome; it brings on all sorts of friction of an unpleasant nature. The more we are reaching out for pleasurable friction, the more we are also running into painful friction of all sorts. But it is not necessary to remain on that level, it is possible to ascend into soul-existence which is frictionless and is the secret place of the most High.

Question: What role does temptation play in all this?

Dr. Hora: Temptation involves us in a phony issue. It gets us involved in ruminating about whether we should or should not indulge in pleasure seeking. This is a false issue and it distracts us from the real issue. What is the real issue? The real issue is frictionless joy. Soul-existence.

The principle of harmonious living is as follows: Take no thought for what should be or what should not be. Seek ye first to know the harmony and joy of soul-existence, the good of God.

Dialogue No. 24

THE HUMAN MOCKERY

Question: I have a question about phoniness. When people are overconfident, we are pretty quick to call them phonies. What makes them so different from people who are fearful or easily intimidated? It seems that fearfulness is considered genuine, while overconfidence is phony.

Dr. Hora: What is the real problem?

Comment: I used to be fearful and now I am overconfident; and it is worse because it seems to be phony. I had a little fear the other day, and it felt like an old friend.

Dr. Hora: Someone said once: "I got so scared when I came here today because I suddenly realized that I forgot to be anxious." All this goes under the heading of "the mockery of human existence." Being human is a mockery. Do you understand that?

Comment: Not enough to laugh.

Dr. Hora: What is this mockery mocking? God's creation. God created a perfect universe and peopled it with perfect spiritual reflections of himself. And look at the human race—it is a mockery.

Question: Don't you have to know something in order to mock it?

Dr. Hora: It is being done through collective conspiracy. The whole human race seems to be conspiring together to make a mockery of God's beautiful, perfect creation. Everything on the human level is a slanderous lie about what really is.

Comment: But nobody is to blame for that.

Dr. Hora: Maybe you are, a little.

Comment: Don't take that personally.

Dr. Hora: What is the value of understanding that the human condition is a mockery of God's perfect creation?

Comment: It protects us from believing the lie that there is no perfection, that there is no God, that there is no truth or goodness.

Comment: Many of our institutions—the school system, the legal system, political organizations—are based on the ignorant acceptance of the human condition as it seems to be.

Comment: I don't think that is true. Certainly, what often is taking place in the educational and the legal systems appears to be a mockery, and may be ludicrous from time to time. But it seems to me that the actual institutions themselves—insofar as any good is evidenced in their outworking—are based on a partial perception of the truth; and the individuals who seem so inspiring in any walk of life are the ones who are somehow able to see the truth, and to work in their professional lives in a guided way.

Dr. Hora: There is one characteristic that is universally believed to be very offensive to people. One hears it frequently said: "I can't stand that guy, he takes himself too seriously." Now isn't it interesting that, if someone takes himself too seriously, we find it objectionable. We could ask: "What is the meaning of such a collective acknowledgement that man is not to take himself seriously or he incurs our disfavor?"

Comment: It occurs to me that if an individual takes himself too seriously, he is not interested in me but in himself, isn't that so?

Dr. Hora: We had a president not long ago who took himself very seriously; he had a very strange appearance. He didn't see the mockery of his own position, he thought he had personal power; consequently, he became humorless, disjointed, and graceless—even his handwriting deteriorated to a significant degree, and his thinking processes tended to become self-contradictory. Apparently, in order to be healthy, it is helpful not to take ourselves too seriously—or anyone else, for that matter.

Comment: Dr. Hora, I don't understand what you mean when you say, taking oneself too seriously.

Dr. Hora: It means believing in what one feels, what one thinks, what one believes, and in everything that seems to be.

When we believe whatever seems to be, we are in trouble.

You brought up the phenomena of overconfidence and timidity, correctly perceiving that neither of them is true. When we call someone a phony, we are accusing him of a deliberate lie or a put-on. As long as man is unenlightened about the human condition, he may be just an innocent liar. For instance, St. Paul said: ". . . every man [is] a liar" (Romans 3:4). And Jesus, speaking of the human race, said: "He is a liar and the father of it" (John 8:44). In other words, it is a mockery because we are not what we seem to be; and we are searching and studying and praying that it might be revealed to us what we really are and what really *is*.

There is a story about a Zen monk who was studying for many years, and one day he got enlightened and he was seized with a laughing cramp, a spasm of laughter. It is recorded that he couldn't stop laughing for two days; he nearly died from it. He probably suddenly saw the mockery of the human condition.

Comment: It nearly killed him, he almost died of laughing.

Comment: There is a story about Lazarus when he was raised from the dead. Some sources claim that, when he came out of the tomb, he looked around and started to laugh uncontrollably.

Comment: After he was raised from the dead, he died laughing.

Dr. Hora: An interesting question could be asked about Lazarus. He died the ordinary human mockery death. According to the Bible, he was dead for four days and then Jesus resurrected him, and he lived for a certain period of time, perhaps many years. Now the question is: "How did he die the second time?" Was it the same as the first time, or was it different?

Question: Is it known?

Dr. Hora: There is no record of it because this is very subjective. However, we can ask the question: "Do enlightened people die the same way as unenlightened people?"

Comment: You once said that they become translated.

Dr. Hora: Enoch was translated, but this is something very close. There must be a difference, don't you think? Wherein lies the difference? Let us try to put it this way: What is the difference between an enlightened individual and an unenlightened individual?

Comment: One knows who he really is, and the other believes he is what he seems to be.

Dr. Hora: Right. Jesus once said that the difference between him and other people was that "I know whence I came, and whither I go; but ye cannot tell whence I come, and whither I go" (John 8: 14).

Comment: And when he dies, the unenlightened man thinks he isn't going to be any more; the enlightened man knows that he is going to be more than what he is.

Dr. Hora: That's very nicely put. If you know that you don't have to take yourself seriously, then dying must be much easier. If we are able not to take ourselves too seriously, that brings a great release, an overall easing of tensions. As we consciously realize that our lives are just a mockery we can really relax and become more peaceful and grateful. It is good to know that the human condition is not to be taken too seriously because it is not what it seems to be.

If we can behold the good of God, then, in juxtaposition, all the evil things of this world begin to fade and appear as less and less frightening, less and less real, and less and less worthy of our mental preoccupations. And of course, one develops a tremendous sense of humor.

Question: Is there a danger of becoming stoical if one doesn't take oneself too seriously?

Dr. Hora: Well, what is stoicism? It is an extreme form of self-righteousness which says: Pain is the most real thing there is and I am going to endure it; I will brace myself against it.

Question: What about the happy-go-lucky man who appears not to be caring about anything, who doesn't take anything seriously?

Question: By the way, what does an enlightened man take seriously?

Dr. Hora: Nothing. Enlightened man is never serious; he is reverential. Seriousness is self-confirmatory. Sometimes, what other people take seriously strikes us as very funny, and what we take seriously may seem funny to someone else. Suppose someone disagrees with what you say. That can turn into a big deal. Suppose someone says: "I don't like your hairdo." This can become a calamity. Nevertheless, it is necessary to be able to communicate meaningfully, in spite of the fact that we are ridiculous.

Comment: But we shouldn't ridicule anybody.

Dr. Hora: Right. We are laughing at the human condition, not at individuals. We have loving, positive regard for one another as spiritual reflections of infinite Love-Intelligence. We communicate reverentially and meaningfully with one another, helping to clarify what really is.

Dialogue No. 25

ETERNAL DAMNATION

Comment: I would like to make a comment: a little bit of prayer goes a long way. This morning a right idea crossed my mind which just made me stand up straight, and off I went to work. Just one little bit of right thinking made the day for me. Before that, I had a restless night and many things seemed to be wrong, but it was all corrected in an instant. This is very amazing to me.

Dr. Hora: Yes, a little prayer, a right idea, can have far-reaching consequences, and amazing things can happen.

Comment: It reminds me again of the idea that if you want to pick up a strand of pearls, all you need to do is to grasp one pearl and the rest will follow.

Dr. Hora: When someone reports something good, and if we can sincerely rejoice with that individual, then we are close to the kingdom of God. Not many people can do that.

Comment: I noticed that in my own life. Sometimes when I hear something good I tend to be very suspicious and it is very difficult for me to be open to that joy.

Dr. Hora: Many people are inclined to feel bad if something good happens to someone else.

Comment: It's a real downer.

Comment: On the other hand, one can reason that if it happens to someone else, it can happen to me also.

Dr. Hora: That requires us to be a little closer to God. Ordinarily, unenlightened man thinks that one man's gain is another's loss. If someone wins a million dollars on the lottery, others may feel impoverished. That is the ignorant way of thinking. But if we have a spiritual perspective on life, everything changes. What blesses one, blesses all. If we understand this principle, we can rejoice in the good of another. This eliminates envy, competition, malice, jealousy. Some even get depressed if they hear of something good happening to another. That's very sad. If we are able to sincerely rejoice in the good of another, that indicates that we have grasped the portent of the spiritual law, which goes as follows: "The law of the Spirit of life in Christ Jesus has made me free from the law of sin and death" (Romans 8:2). What is the law of sin and death? The law of sin and death is what we are talking about, namely, the idea that one man's gain is another man's loss. But the law of the Spirit says, what blesses one, blesses all. The understanding of this law has far-reaching consequences. Once we understand it, we can really afford to be loving. It may seem funny and strange, but some people are afraid to expend energy on kindness; they are afraid that they will be shortchanged, that they won't get back as much kindness as they expend. There are people who are afraid to smile lest someone might refuse to smile back.

Comment: In the school where I teach, everybody believes that it is important to be sad and grumpy.

Dr. Hora: Ordinarily, if our thinking is according to the law of sin and death, we do not dare to be generous, we do not dare to be loving, and if something good comes our way, we do not dare to talk about it lest someone hate us for being happy.

Comment: It sounds sick.

Dr. Hora: In certain circles it is customary to complain about how bad things are. This is an act of kindness toward one's neighbor, who will feel good if we feel bad.

Once I worked with a man who thought he was suffering from depression. As we were sitting and talking, it came out that he was not really depressed, he was only afraid that people might want to borrow money from him, or ask him a favor. So he developed a habit of making a sad face so that no one would ask anything of him. The long face was his protection against having to be generous. This is the law of sin and death; but the law of the Spirit of life, according to the teachings of Christ Jesus, is that what blesses one, bleses all. If we are happy, we share it and are grateful.

Question: In the kingdom of God is everybody equal?

Dr. Hora: In the kingdom of God there is no equality whatsoever.

Question: Individuality?

Dr. Hora: That's right. Everyone is a precious, unique individual expression of God's infinite goodness. And there is no way that one could be compared with another, or measured against another. Take for instance a maple tree. A maple tree has millions of leaves, and every leaf is different from all the others. There are no two leaves alike among millions of leaves. How are we going to measure which maple leaf is superior or inferior, or more important or less important than the others? It is ridiculous, when you think of it. There is absolutely no equality, and that's a glorious freedom. The whole idea of equality is existentially invalid. Every individual is an expression of God. Naïve people assume that equality means justice. Equality is not justice, love is justice. The Christly justice is as follows: "Love your enemies, bless them that curse you, do good to them that hate you, and pray for them which despitefully use you, and persecute you" (Matthew 5:44). Some may think this is impractical and even absurd.

Comment: It is hard to see that this does not mean being a doormat, a masochist, or self-destructive. When you say this, I immediately see myself as a victim of abuse.

Comment: I guess when people are destructive toward us we can pray for them because we can imagine the burden they are carrying.

Dr. Hora: You just said that one can console oneself with the thought of how miserably the aggressor must feel. That's not the point.

Comment: If we accept the proposition that nothing comes into experience uninvited, then we realize that persecution and victimization are tailor-made problems for our edification. And if one can discern the meaning of what seems to be, there is great potential for growth.

Dr. Hora: What is this process called? It is prayer. That is what Jesus meant when he said: "Pray for them which despitefully use you, and persecute you."

Here we have to consider a very important point: We can-not use God to solve our problems for us. In prayer we use our problems to come closer to God. Our problems are op-portunities which show us where we have to come closer to God. There is great value and comfort in understanding that our problems are tailor-made lessons to teach us what we need to know. If we don't understand this, we can find prayer very frustrating. We often make the mistake of trying to use God to serve us. If we could do that, we would be greater than God, and God would be our servant. It is frequently assumed that in prayer we tell God what he should do; but of course, this does not work. Problems are telling us what we need to know in order to come into better alignment with the divine Principle, with the law of the Spirit of life in Christ Jesus. And then the problems disappear.

Sometimes a problem can be a turning point in one's life if it is healed through understanding its meaning. One can actually be reborn of the Spirit in this manner. Every problem is tailor-made and has a purpose. The purpose is to bring us closer to God. And if we are willing to come closer to God, more in line with divine Principle, not only does the problem disappear but we have ascended to a higher level of spiritual consciousness and we have been greatly blessed.

Question: Is it possible to lose the understanding which we have gained?

Dr. Hora: It is possible to deceive ourselves into believing that we already know when we don't really know. Once we have really understood a problem, that problem will never recur. There may arise other problems which, in turn, would indicate other areas of thought which need to be brought in line with divine reality. Life is a school where we are given problems to solve. There is such a thing as eternal damnation. What do you think it is?

Comment: It is when you die and go to hell and stay there forever. But you must have something else in mind; I guess it would not apply here.

Dr. Hora: You are right. It would not apply here. It means failing to learn from our mistakes and repeating them over and over and over again. There are some who spend thirty, forty, or fifty years running into the same problem again and again, and they never learn from it. I know a young lady who has had a half a dozen engagements. She gets engaged to be married, and it always fizzles out the same way. Now there must be something there which she needs to learn, because this thing keeps repeating itself according to the same pattern. This can go on ad infinitum if we don't learn the meaning of it and correct it. And that is what we mean by eternal damnation. Eternal damnation is not necessary. Problems are inevitable, but eternal damnation is not.

Question: What is the meaning of endless complaining?

Comment: It seems to be an interest in self-assertion or self-confirmation.

Dr. Hora: When a form of misery becomes pleasurable due to its self-confirmatory content, then we have a situation ripe for eternal damnation because one enjoys the problem.

Question: Do people enjoy the pain or the meaning of the pain?

Dr. Hora: The meaning. There are so-called chronic complainers.

Comment: It occurs to me that there is a very simple antidote to complaining, and that is gratitude.

Dr. Hora: What is the healing remedy to chronic complaining and to eternal damnation? The Zen Master has one remedy. He says: "Erase yourself utterly." What does he mean?

Comment: Turn your attention completely to God instead of to yourself.

Dr. Hora: There are certain problems which are more self-confirmatory than painful. They are tolerable through self-confirmation and there is no interest in being healed. This can go on and on eternally. Complaining and self-pity are two frequent problems which have a high degree of self-confirmatory content, and therefore there is little incentive to be healed.

Question: Does that refer to the quotation from the Bible that men love darkness?

Dr. Hora: Yes.

Comment: It seems that there is an incredible amount of stupidity involved here, because self-confirmation is self-destruction, and it would seem that an intelligent individual would want to abandon that.

Dr. Hora: What do you think suicide is? Suicide is the ultimate form of self-confirmation. "I can kill myself, therefore I am."

Dialogue No. 26

WHAT IS THE PURPOSE OF MAN?

Question: What does it mean if we don't enjoy certain types of work?

Dr. Hora: When it comes to enjoying work, it is helpful to recall the story of the two happy Zen monks. People asked these monks: "What is the secret of your joy and happiness?" They answered: "Isn't it marvelous to chop wood and carry water all day long?" There is a special meaning to this kind of an answer. What is it?

Comment: Gratefulness for the ability to do that?

Dr. Hora: That could be an interpretation of it, but there is more to it.

Comment: The issue is not chopping wood or carrying water but being happy regardless of the nature of the activity.

Dr. Hora: The idea is that when one is in Christ-consciousness, even the most menial task or chore is an occasion for rejoicing and being happy. We don't get happiness from people or from things or from activities; we bring happiness to our activities, to people, to things, and to situations. Unenlightened man is trying to get something out of his activities and out of people; he has a "getting" kind of orientation toward life. Enlightened man sees himself as an expression of the good of God. He is a channel through whom the good of God flows into all aspects of life. It is like reversing the movement of the celestial bodies. When we are ignorant of astronomy, we have the impression that the sun is revolving around the earth and the earth is the center of the universe. But when we learn a little bit about astronomy we are told that, contrary to appearances, the sun is not rising in the East and traveling around the earth and setting in the West, but it is the other way around. The earth is revolving around the sun, the sun is stationary. So enlightened man sees life completely reversed—right side up. He is not seeing life as getting something out of the world for himself, but as letting something flow into the world through himself.

Question: Is man needed?

Dr. Hora: Of course, what would be the universe without man? This is a ridiculous but necessary question. It cannot be answered. Just as the sun is inconceivable and unknowable without the sunbeam, so God and the universe is inconceivable without man. We are what is. And happiness is not something we can get. Man is not here to get happiness from life. Man is here to manifest the happiness of God, which already is. We tend to be frustrated most of the time because we cannot get from the world what we want to get. But if we discover that there is nothing to get but everything to give, there is a tremendous revolution taking place in our outlook. "As thou seest, so thou beest."

The natural, unenlightened way to live is to seek ego-gratification, which means desiring to feel good. Now what is the alternative to the natural way? It is the enlightened way, which means to seek existential fulfillment. What does that mean?

Comment: Self-esteem.

Dr. Hora: No, self-esteem is a by-product of fulfillment. What could be more important in life than a desire to feel good?

Comment: Being what God is.

Comment: Being a beneficial presence in the world.

Dr. Hora: Existential fulfillment means fulfilling the purpose for which we have been created. Will that make us feel good? What will we get out of it?

Comment: We will be happy, healthy, and satisfied.

Dr. Hora: Right. So existential fulfillment means being what we are meant to be. What more can one ask?

Question: What are we meant to be?

Comment: I am always thinking about what I should be, and that way I never know what I am meant to be. And that's not a very happy situation.

Dr. Hora: Sometimes, when we don't know what we are meant to be, we are asking other people, or we are looking around to find out what other people want us to be. In such a case we are concerned with trying to please or to displease someone. When we try to please or displease someone, we are looking to him to find out what he wants us to be, and then we will either want to be what he wants us to be, or we will not. And so we get hooked on something invalid.

Question: What does the term "meant to be" mean? What is there that we are uniquely and individually meant to be?

Dr. Hora: That's a good question. How can we know for sure that there is such a thing as a purpose for man? Unenlightened man has a depressed mental horizon; he cannot conceive of anything coming from a level higher than the top of the head of the tallest man in his visual field. He cannot go higher. The assumption is that every rule, every law, every moral idea must come from another human brain. Therefore, he rightfully questions and is skeptical. This is called moral relativism. Without God nothing is really absolutely valid, everything becomes relative. And if everything is relative, anything goes.

Comment: One of my friends, who is the mother of a child, has recently divorced her husband and is at present living with a woman. I was just amazed to hear that.

Dr. Hora: Yes, that's one of the examples of moral relativism. If the moral principles are man-made, then nothing is absolutely valid, anything goes. As long as our mental outlook on life is horizontal, we are living in chaos, or in the tyranny of trends. Which means that the lowest common denominator is accepted as a standard. What is the lowest common denominator in ignorant thinking?

Comment: Feeling good.

Dr. Hora: Right. The majority of people want to feel good; therefore, this is the primary moral law. Whatever will make one feel good, that is good and that will then be the basic assumption of what is right. The extreme form of this ignorance is drug addiction. A drug addict seeks to feel good at any price. A well-known television star used to end her show regularly by saying: "And remember folks, if you feel like doing it, do it!"

Question: What about people who just feel bad all the time?

Dr. Hora: There is a form of feeling bad which is a form of feeling good. What do we call that?

Comment: Masochism.

Comment: Melancholy.

Dr. Hora: It is called self-pity. Self-pity is a way of feeling good about feeling bad. However, we are here to consider the meaning and purpose of individual existence because fulfillment, health, happiness, wisdom, harmony can only come if one is fulfilling the meaning and purpose for which one is created. Unenlightened man might say: "My parents created me, I am going to ask them." And there are some parents who say: "I created you, and therefore you are for the purpose for which I have created you." A father used to say to his son, a grown man: "So how come I am not getting any pleasure out of you?" It didn't even occur to him that perhaps this question might not be valid.

How can we know for sure that there is a purpose and a meaning to our individual lives, and that this purpose and this meaning is built in by the Creator?

Comment: Some people say that individuals have special aptitudes.

Dr. Hora: Did God want you to be an air conditioning engineer? Do you think that that's what God had in mind for you? What does God know about air conditioning?

Comment: I heard an analogy which says that the light beam fulfills its specific purpose at the point where it hits a blade of grass or a flower. But I don't really understand it.

Dr. Hora: This is a beautiful analogy, except for the fact that the light beam has the great advantage of not having the capability of ignorance. A light beam is incapable of being dark. But man seems to be able to shed darkness and to live in darkness, at least experientially. In that respect we are unique among the life forms on this planet.

Comment: It seems possible for us to be what we are not.

Dr. Hora: Right.

Comment: In our capability to be ignorant there is implied a capability of being conscious.

Dr. Hora: There is such a thing as the principle of existential validation, and Jesus formulated it this way: "By their fruits ye shall know them" (Matthew 7:20). When we are fulfilling our mission in life, we are healthy, we are happy, we are good, we are harmonious, we are beautiful, we are intelligent, and we are the "salt of the earth." "But if the salt have lost his savour, wherewith shall it be salted? it is thenceforth good for nothing, but to be cast out, and to be trodden under foot of men" (Matthew 5:13). That means that if we are ignorant of our true meaning and purpose in life, we live in ignorance, and the consequences of this ignorance bear poor fruit. So the principle of existential validation makes it possible for us to know whether we are on the beam with the purpose of divine intent for us, or whether we are off the beam. When we are on the beam, we bear good fruit, and we are the "salt of the earth," a beneficial presence in the world.

Dialogue No. 27

WHAT IS LIFE?

Question: What is the difference between the two versions of the first commandment? According to your version: Thou shalt have no other interests before the good of God; and according to the Biblical version: Thou shalt have no other gods before me.

Dr. Hora: You mean what is the advantage of reformulating the first commandment the way we did?

Comment: It is more meaningful because, if you are interested in the good of God, then you are automatically paying attention. So it seems to me to be a more meaningful statement to make to myself rather than the church-type commandment.

Dr. Hora: That's the right point. You see, the original formulation has a religious flavor. But, when we say thou shalt have no other interests before the good of God, this is more meaningful nowadays.

Comment: It is easier to catch yourself in the act of worshiping false goods.

Dr. Hora: Right. And it is not a religious statement; it is an epistemological statement. What is the meaning of that?

Comment: Having to do with the nature of knowledge.

Dr. Hora: Right. It brings to our attention the fact that the real issue is right knowing. When we say thou shalt have no other gods, it doesn't refer to knowledge, it refers to emotions, to sentiment. But when we deal with channeling our interests, then we are talking about what is going to have an impact on our thinking. An epistemological statement has greater validity for us.

Question: Is the same true of Jesus' formulation of the first commandment?

Dr. Hora: Yes. He said: "Thou shalt love the Lord thy God

with all thy heart, and with all thy soul, and with all thy mind" (Matthew 22:37; Mark 12:30,33; Luke 10:27). Here we are exhorted to exert ourselves in every possible way to love God. But to love God can be misinterpreted because, when people hear the word "love," they immediately think of feelings. Then emotionalism enters into it, and we know what emotionalism has done in religion. Religion is mostly emotional (except for the Jesuits and the Talmudists; with them it seems to be intellectual). But for us it is epistemologically existential. Who can explain this term? Who can give reasons why?

Comment: "Wise men never try . . ."

Dr. Hora: Epistemologically, existential means that right knowing has relevancy to our being; we can even say that being is right knowing, and right knowing is being. Most people believe that life is experience. It is a common assumption that if we have had many experiences, it means that we have lived a lot, that the more experiences we have had, the more we have lived. We travel here and we travel there; we try this and we try that; and we are looking to experience as much as possible and to learn from experience. And then we say that we have lived a lot. So the prevalent thinking is that living means experiencing things. Who would dare to say no to that?

Comment: Except that all the time, while we are having all those experiences, we are haunted by the question: "Is this all there is to life?"

Dr. Hora: Yes, and it drives one to seek more and more exciting experiences. Who would dare to say that life is not an experience? Let us ask this, What are experiences?

Comment: They are dreams.

Dr. Hora: Yes, they are dreams. Do you really understand this?

Comment: Sometimes I do.

Dr. Hora: All experiences are dreams, and we spend our lives chasing after a better dream. Now if life is not an exerience, what is it?

Comment: It is goodness; it is being aware of the goodness that already is.

Dr. Hora: Isn't that an experience?

Comment: No. It is a goodness that you are aware of.

Dr. Hora: What is life?

Question: Would it be meaningful to say that life is God?

Dr. Hora: For him to whom it is meaningful, it is meaningful. Life is God. Is it meaningful to anyone here?

Comment: I would say that it is our consciousness of being.

Dr. Hora: How could we find this more meaningful?

Comment: Perhaps by considering certain aspects of life, such as goodness, happiness, beauty, love, peace.

Dr. Hora: That's life. Life is not experiential; life is epistemological, spiritual. Life is knowing, knowing is being. What would happen if today, right here, we all came to the realization that life is not an experience? What would happen to us?

Comment: Our interests would immediately change.

Dr. Hora: Right. The first commandment would become actualized right here. It would be very easy for us to live within the context of the first commandment. It is difficult to live within the context of the first commandment as long as we cherish experiences. That's what makes it so difficult; it is difficult to be interested in the good of God if we are interested in something else.

Question: Does this invalidate the educational concept of experiential learning in children?

Dr. Hora: It does not invalidate it, it just puts it into a different dimension. As long as we are learning to be human, it is necessary to have experiences. But we are already leaving that behind; we are saying good-bye to the world of dreams and reaching for reality.

Comment: But then we don't stop having experiences, we learn to transcend them.

Dr. Hora: When a child is born, he has to learn first how to live in unreality; for this he needs to be educated experientially until his education will result in a crisis, or more crises. And then he will want to be liberated from his education and discover reality; reality, which is not experiential but which is knowing the good of God. Now, when we understand that life is entirely apart from the world of experiences, we begin to lose interest in most of the things our friends and enemies are interested in. And that is called ascension. We are rising higher and higher in consciousness, and gradually losing interest in many, many things which used to be very important to us. Things like compliments, praise, status, fame, power, possessions, and all sorts of things. Real life is entirely separate from the world of dreams, which is called experiencing.

When we wake up in the morning after eight hours of dreaming, there is a separation between that state of consciousness and the awakened one. Anyone can see that when a dreamer wakes up in the morning, he leaves his dreams behind; he doesn't concern himself anymore with what he was dreaming about, and he starts the day. There seems to be some difference between night dreaming and daytime experiencing. Similarly, there is a significant difference between experiential living and the discovery of real life. It is as if we had awakened again. The Bible tells us to awake and realize the Christ-consciousness which will illumine our life. What is this Christ-consciousness? It is the knowledge that life is God.

Now the question is: "Will these experiences continue after we have understood this total separation?" Yes, just as everybody goes to sleep even if he is not interested in dreaming. The less we are interested in our dreams and experiences, the healthier we shall be. So we come back to the first commandment, which says: Thou shalt have no other interests before the good of God, which is spiritual, not experiential.

A Zen Master was asked how enlightenment could protect one from the heat of the summer and the cold of the winter. He said: "In the summer we swelter, in the winter we freeze." Now what's so smart about that?

Comment: We just don't make a federal case of our experiences.

Dr. Hora: Right. The point of the Zen Master's answer is that you shouldn't make a fuss about how you feel, it is not important. In other words, we can have any kind of experiences we want as long as we are not interested in them.

Question: But what do you do with these experiences if it is impossible not to have them?

Comment: It seems to me that it is possible to classify experiences as necessary and unnecessary, and that the unnecessary ones are the indulgences, and obviously we learn from these experiences. For instance, if I drink alcohol, I will suffer until I learn from the experiences and lose interest in it. Experiences such as eating and sleeping and going to the bathroom are necessary, but we don't have to be involved with them mentally.

Dr. Hora: That's very good. But, in general, the point of the first commandment is that there has to come a shift in interest, and it is not easy to lose interest in experiences, especially pleasurable ones, and become interested in something as illusive as PAGL. You cannot smell it, you cannot taste it, you cannot touch it, you cannot feel it, and here we are interested in something as evanescent as that—more even than in sex. And that's difficult. But if we come to understand what life really is in juxtaposition to experiencing it becomes easier, and we gradually develop a more intelligent attitude toward our experiences.

A headache, for instance, is an experience. Some people suffer more from headaches—or colds, menstruation, backaches, coughs, etc.—than other people. Some people don't make a federal case of it, while others get involved with their experiences, exacerbate them, and go from bad to worse. I think it was the famous physician Selye who said: "Disease is not the problem but the patient's attitude toward the disease is the problem." We can learn to have an intelligent attitude toward experiences, namely, total disinterest, which is not synonymous with denial. We are not denying these experiences, but we are not going to get involved with them if we understand the first commandment.

Question: Should we ignore them?

Dr. Hora: One thing we must never do is ignore anything. The Zen Master didn't say to ignore the heat of the summer or the cold of the winter. We would get frostbite if we ignored the cold. He said: "Don't make a federal case out of how you feel." Have an intelligent attitude toward experiences, neither ignore them nor exaggerate their importance. Our primary interest is in life, which is not an experience but a reality.

Question: What about art and the theater?

Dr. Hora: Now there is a general erroneous belief that the right thing to do is to get deeply and emotionally involved with everything. If someone sees a movie, for instance—nowadays there are panic movies like *The Exorcist*—and the viewer is vomiting during the performance, that is considered good; or when someone gets hysterical during a show, that is considered good. It is a good show and a good audience; one has good, honest-to-goodness experiences if one gets involved with the show. That's what the directors and producers of shows are trying to achieve—to provide the audience with a powerful experience. Which means to get them hypnotized. And, of course, that's how ordinary, normal people go to the movies and the theater. Sometimes they may be sick for weeks after a show. The only way to go to see a movie or a show is to preserve a healthy distance, and to be an observer rather than a participant, because we know that, contrary to general belief, life is not an experience.

Question: Don't people sometimes speak of experiencing beauty and love and joy? Is that just a loose way of thinking?

Dr. Hora: Right.

Question: Wouldn't one be experiencing beauty through an art form?

Dr. Hora: Sometimes people talk about paintings in terms of how these paintings make them feel. That's a masturbatory perspective. We don't understand art with our feelings.

Comment: That brings to mind the crucifixion, which is something detestable when you look at it as experience. It is hard to look at the crucifixion without seeing it as an experience. But Jesus wanted people to realize something rather than experience something.

Dr. Hora: That's the tragedy of Christianity, that people saw the crucifixion as a sado-masochistic experience, an obscene and bloody act. Whereas it was meant to be a demonstration of the irrelevancy of experience and the indestructibility of life.

Dialogue No. 28

OVERCOMING THE WORLD

Comment: Today I had a wonderful sense of coming here with a desire to be a beneficial presence in the world.

Dr. Hora: Ordinarily, people are struggling to present a healthy appearance in order to be socially acceptable. This is called pretending, and it is a sickness in itself. On the other hand, when people go to a doctor they want to show how sick they are. And so we go to the doctor so that he can see how sick we are, and when we return to a social situation we want people to see how healthy we are. In either case we are lying. We are lying when we are pretending to be healthy and we are lying when we are claiming to be sick. In other words, ordinary life is a constant lie. When we say we come here healthy which lie are we perpetrating?

Comment: No lie.

Dr. Hora: Would you explain that?

Comment: When we claim to come here healthy, we are spiritually minded.

Dr. Hora: In other words, we have a special concept of health which seems to be entirely different from what is generally thought of as health. In what way is it different?

Comment: I was thinking about the verse we have discussed here before: "If thine eye be single, thy whole body shall be full of light" (Matthew 6:22). We have discussed this in the context of Jesus' definition of health, and how curious it is that he refers to a healthy body as light—meaning understanding.

Dr. Hora: Right. In other words, when we say that we come here healthy, we mean that we are preparing our thoughts to be directed toward God, toward spiritual values. And when our eye is single, our outlook on life becomes focused in the direction of one God; we find ourselves coming here healthy and in search of healing. That seems paradoxical, doesn't it?

Comment: No. We seek healing so that our health might be permanent.

Dr. Hora: So then we have defined health as spiritual mindedness. And how could we define healing?

Comment: Immunity from all distractions.

Dr. Hora: Yes, so that we may be whole all the time.

Comment: Recently, I have been very distracted and mentally preoccupied with a family in our neighborhood which was afflicted by a series of tragedies. I caught myself trying to figure out why it happened to them and who was to blame for it. And I also thought that I would like to know the answers to these questions so that my family would be protected from such a fate.

Dr. Hora: What is the flaw in this reasoning?

Comment: She is asking two of the six futile questions.

Dr. Hora: What are the six futile questions?

Comment: 1. What's wrong? 2. How do you feel? 3. Why? 4. Who is to blame? 5. What should we do? 6. How should we do it?

Dr. Hora: What is the meaning of the six futile questions? First of all, they don't solve anything. But essentially the meaning of these questions is that they imply that man is an independent entity, apart from God.

Comment: I don't understand the difference between a meaning and a cause.

Dr. Hora: What is the meaning of meaning?

Comment: Meaning sheds light. It reveals the nature of what the issue at hand is.

Comment: Dr. Hora defined it previously as the mental equivalent of what seems to be.

Dr. Hora: Right. What is a mental equivalent? It is a thought which underlies a phenomenon.

Comment: Could you please give us an example?

Dr. Hora: Yes. If we think that man is an independent entity, entirely apart from God, then this thought will inevitably express itself in any of the six futile questions. It will not cause these questions but will manifest itself in them. Ignorance doesn't have a cause, it has a meaning. Many people have difficulty in understanding the difference between cause and meaning. What is the meaning of this difficulty? Ignorant man is judging by appearances. For instance, if an apple falls down from a tree, ignorant man will say that the wind was blowing and that caused the apple to fall down from the tree. Or he will say that a truck was passing by and shook the ground, this shook the tree and the apple fell. Or he will say that the apple was ripe and got too heavy and the stem dried up and that's why it fell down. This is cause-and-effect reasoning; and the way we see things with our eyes makes it natural to think this way. This seems natural and logical, except that it is not quite true. If the apple falls down from the tree, it reveals the existence of an invisible force called gravitation. So it has a meaning. The apple falling from the tree has a meaning rather than a cause. And as long as we think in terms of cause and effect, we have the dubious distinction of being narrow-minded. Jesus called it judging by appearances. All ignorance —everywhere in the universe—comes from judging by appearances.

Question: Does an apple have a purpose?

Dr. Hora: Sometimes we speak of purpose instead of cause. Purpose is a teleological cause.

Comment: Just imagine how long we would have to be coming here if we were not warned against using these futile questions.

Dr. Hora: Eternally. Consider how long it took the human race to evolve to a point where a Newton appeared on the scene and asked the right question about a simple phenomenon like a falling apple. Can you imagine how many people before Newton have seen apples fall from trees? None of them asked a meaningful question about it. Newton was the first to ask: "What does this occurence reveal? What is the meaning of it?"

Comment: I was always of the impression that he is credited for having given cause-and-effect thinking a great leap forward.

Dr. Hora: That would not be surprising.

Comment: But even this is just an analogy because it deals with a physical law, whereas we are seeking to understand spiritual reality.

Dr. Hora: Yes, that is true. But cause-and-effect thinking has been discredited even in physics, notably by Heisenberg with his Nobel prize-winning theory of indeterminacy.

Question: If we cannot reason why, and we cannot judge by appearances, there must be an entirely different way of knowing. What is it?

Dr. Hora: All right. Let us ask: "What happened to Newton at the moment when he noticed the apple fall. What hit him?" He wasn't hit by the apple, he was hit by inspired wisdom, creative intelligence.

Comment: Or heightened perceptivity.

Dr. Hora: Jesus said: "In the world ye shall have tribulation: but be of good cheer; I have overcome the world" (John 16:33). What is the relevancy of this statement to what we were just talking about? Once we learn to rise above the six futile questions and ask the two intelligent questions, we have overcome the world. We have entered into another dimension of reality and everything is different in that moment. In what way is the world of the two intelligent questions different from the world of the six futile questions? In the world of the futile questions there is tribulation. Contrariwise, the world of the intelligent questions is characterized by harmony, understanding, peace, assurance, gratitude, and love.

Comment: Would you please tell us the two intelligent questions again?

Dr. Hora: Certainly. The first is: "What is the meaning of what seems to be?" And the second is: "What is what really *is?*" These constitute a double doorway at the entrance to the kingdom of God.

Dialogue No. 29

AMBITION

Question: Is it possible to live and be successful without ambition?

Question: What do you mean by successful?

Dr. Hora: There are three frequent afflictions which people tend to suffer from: pride, ambition, and vanity. It is hard to measure which of these is worse, but it would seem that ambition is the most troublesome.

Question: Does ambition include negative ambition, like being a bum?

Dr. Hora: Yes. How would we define ambition?

Comment: Wanting to be the best of something, I guess.

Dr. Hora: Not necessarily. Actually, it is healthy to want to be the best possible.

Question: How about the greatest?

Dr. Hora: These are subdivisions of ambition.

Comment: Ambition is self-confirmatory. You set yourself goals.

Comment: It is a thought of what should be.

Dr. Hora: Exactly. And it is full of frustration because if one succeeds, one gets sicker; and if one fails, one also gets sicker. We have to be very careful about ambition. Ambition is an existentially invalid idea.

Question: Is it not based on a desire to be worthy? A false way of establishing self-worth?

Dr. Hora: In certain cases it can be so.

Question: Is there spiritual ambition?

Dr. Hora: Yes, that's very dangerous. To be ambitious in the spiritual dimension of thought is a self-contradictory position to take, and it is self-defeating.

Comment: It is also all-consuming because, in order to be ambitious, one has to fantasize a great deal. One is constantly involved with one's own thoughts. It is a real trap.

Dr. Hora: Right.

Comment: Someone who is ambitious to be enlightened might wind up labeling himself as "enlightened."

Comment: When we are ambitious, we are setting ourselves apart from God.

Dr. Hora: Right. It is not easy to be healed of ambition, because the desire to be free of ambition can be an ambition in itself.

Question: Can one think of getting ahead unambitiously, in a right way?

Dr. Hora: Getting ahead of whom?

Comment: In the business world, for instance. Moving up on the ladder.

Dr. Hora: What ladder? In other words, how can you eat your cake and have it, too? What is the alternative to ambition?

Comment: Aspiration.

Dr. Hora: That is just a word.

Comment: To me it is a word, but to you it is probably an alternative.

Comment: The opposite of ambition would be aspiring for nothingness. It's sort of a weird idea. If you are nothing and totally transparent to the will of God, how could you have a desire to excel in a field and climb a ladder?

Comment: We can desire to be more beneficial through greater understanding.

Comment: But one can do that ambitiously.

Comment: I suffer from ambition and reap the consequences thereof. And it seems to me that the alternative to ambition is to completely let go of what I think I should be or should be doing. It reminds me of the story of the young rich man who wanted to follow Jesus and was told to give up everything he cherished. And he couldn't do it. It's hard for me to let God do his will through me.

Comment: Most of the time we think that the alternative to ambition inevitably is failure, but that's not true.

Comment: It's very hard to be aware of being ambitious, to monitor one's consciousness.

Comment: Sometimes when I try not to be ambitious, I become a patsy and allow people to take advantage of me.

Dr. Hora: Pollyanna says everything is good, even while people trample on her. Enlightened man says everything real is good, and the unreal is not worth talking about. It is nothing. So what is the alternative to ambition? How can we survive in a competitive society if we are not going to be ambitious?

Comment: First we have to know that God is our employer. I think that would be a big help.

Dr. Hora: But then wouldn't we be nagging God for a raise or a promotion?

Comment: We don't survive in a competitive society; we live above it. We are not really part of the competitive society if we truly know that we don't need to be ambitious, and that God is the only life. Then there is no competitive society.

Comment: I was recently on a vacation trip and things were going from bad to worse. I felt dejected and responsible because I thought I wasn't being a beneficial presence. And then, in a moment of reflection, a line from the Bible came to me: "The battle is not yours but God's" (II Chronicles 20:15), and it was as if a cloud had lifted. From then on things became harmonious, and seemingly impossible problems resolved themselves in beautiful and surprising ways.

Dr. Hora: Ambition can also sneak into prayer. We can pray ambitiously, and then we are very frustrated that God is not doing his thing. How can that be avoided?

Question: By not trying to succeed?

Comment: That would be negative ambition.

Dr. Hora: What is existential success?

Comment: Trouble-free life.

Dr. Hora: What do you mean?

Comment: Free of illness, friction, and frustration—fulfillment.

Comment: It must be more than just the absence of problems.

Comment: I would say that existential success is when Christ-consciousness is fully realized in us, and that which we thought we were is dead.

Dr. Hora: "I live; yet not I, but Christ liveth in me" (Galatians 2:20).

Comment: It seems to me that gratitude is a very important antidote to ambition.

Dr. Hora: That's a very good point. Furthermore, we need to gain a clear understanding of who we are and what we are. We are nothing, but this nothingness is a beholder. Isn't that interesting?

Man is a certain invisible mysterious consciousness which is capable of beholding the presence and the activity of infinite Mind. About two weeks ago, I was walking in the forest and I dropped an assembly of two little screws which fell apart and disappeared among the leaves. I started kicking the leaves around, but it immediately occurred to me that the harder I searched, the more impossible it would be to find the screws. So I decided not to look for it. God is all-seeing Mind; this Mind can see where those screws are. I am part of this Mind; therefore, this Mind can help me see what it sees. So I just stood there quietly. As I became more and more quiet, my eyes were drawn to a spot about two feet away from me and there, among the leaves, I saw a little metal object glistening. I picked it up. It was part of the screw assembly. So I said, "Thank you God. If you could show me this one, you can also show me the remaining part because you are the all-seeing Mind and I am part of you." So I was standing there quietly, and the same thing happened again. My eye was drawn almost involuntarily to another place about two feet away from the first spot, and again, among the leaves, I found the second part. Now if this had been just one part, someone could say, it was just an accident. But it happened twice in a row, and so it is safe to say that it was a demonstration of a principle. The moment we are willing to become nothing, we become part of that all-seeing, all-knowing presence, the divine Mind, and whatever is needed at that moment, appears.

Comment: The psalmist says: "Be still, and know that I am God" (Psalms 46:10).

Dr. Hora: In prayer we are seeking to behold God. The screws were not important, but the proof of the possibility of becoming aware of God's presence as all-seeing, all-acting Mind was the real treasure. A beholder is always seeking to behold the good of God as omnipresent. This covers the whole issue of life. There is no need to be ambitious. Ambition would have resulted in frustration and in failure to find the screws, but the prayer of beholding is beautiful, easy, and uplifting. Man is thus revealed to be a consciousness capable of becoming conscious of God.

Dialogue No. 30

THE GATEKEEPER

Question: Can one be more enlightened at some times and less enlightened at others? Or relatively more ignorant at times? Or is it all or nothing?

Dr. Hora: Sometimes it is very dark at night and sometimes it is not so dark; it makes a difference. What exactly is your problem?

Comment: I hear that this idea of the final giving up of personal mind is very hard to do and that it is painful.

Dr. Hora: It is only difficult to give up that which you believe you have; what you don't have is not difficult to give up. Right?

Comment: I think of the Book of Revelation, which supposedly describes human consciousness reaching out for enlightenment and experiencing this awful holocaust. It is not a process of increasing peace and harmony.

Dr. Hora: The writer of the Book of Revelation had a very vivid imagination, and he exaggerated his imagery and painted fantastic pictures and symbolic visions. Nowadays he would be labeled a schizophrenic. We must not be afraid to read this book, but we must not use it as an excuse for discouragement, because not everyone has to have such imagination. It is also possible to come to understand God without any fireworks, just very simply and quietly and gratefully.

Comment: Isaiah wrote about attaining an understanding of God: "For precept must be upon precept, precept upon precept; line upon line, line upon line; here a little, and there a little" (Isaiah 28:10).

Dr. Hora: Sometimes we are just looking for an excuse to feel discouraged. We like to hang on to our cherished hangups and we use many rationalizations in order not to part with them.

Question: Dr. Hora, recently our neighborhood has been invaded by derelicts. In view of the fact that you claim that nothing comes into our lives uninvited, I wonder whether we have in any way invited this into our lives.

Dr. Hora: Correction, nothing comes into our *experience* uninvited. Experience is not synonymous with life, even though people fail to make this distinction. When they think of their lives, they think of their experiences. Life is God, the principle of infinite good, of harmony and joy, vitality and vigor, love, beauty, and freedom—that is life. What are experiences? Experiences have nothing to do with life. Would you believe that? How is that possible? What other people consider the very essence of life we have the boldness to claim has nothing to do with life!

Comment: Life is reality, experience is illusion or dream. Therefore, the two have nothing in common.

Dr. Hora: Experiences are dreams.

Question: Do they always involve the five senses?

Dr. Hora: Yes. And imagination and thoughts. Experiences are perceptualized thoughts. What does that mean? They are thoughts which we translate into perceptions. In other words, they are hallucinations. Experiences are our own thoughts coming to us in the form of sensory perceptions. What is a dream? Dreams are thoughts in the form of pictures, images; and experiences are thoughts in the form of sensory perceptions. So life is one thing, and experiences are another.

Comment: Many people talk about experiencing life but, in the light of what you just said, this is impossible. Right?

Dr. Hora: Right. We cannot experience life, we can only experience our thoughts. Life can only be realized.

Question: Do we ever experience someone else's thoughts?

Dr. Hora: We can share other people's thoughts, and we can also share their experiences. Friendships are based on shared experiences because a friend is someone who agrees with us about certain thoughts that we cherish. Enmity is when we disagree. But life is a bird of a different feather.

Question: How can we know that experiences are dreams?

Dr. Hora: If we come to see the validity of the principle that nothing comes into experience uninvited, we can gain a clear understanding of the fact that thought precedes experience. Whatever our mental preoccupations are, they will appear in our experiences in one way or another.

If we want to be beneficial presences in the world, we shall be concerned with seeing the perfect harmony of divine reality everywhere. And when we realize life, we will be able to see the good of God everywhere. And when evil comes to our attention, we shall know that it is only a phenomenon, that is, an appearance. Appearances appear and disappear; they come to our attention but they are not in our experience.

Question: Can't we learn from experience?

Dr. Hora: Sure. That's what education is—learning from experience. And, until we seek enlightenment, we all want to be well-educated people.

Question: Can the good of God be experienced?

Dr. Hora: No, the good of God is realized. Unenlightened man is forever seeking to find better and better experiences.

Comment: I read somewhere that Gandhi refused to write his autobiography because that would have required him to describe his life experiences.

Dr. Hora: The greatest autobiographical work ever written was written by Dante Alighieri. It is entitled *The Divine Comedy (La Divina Comedia)*, and it consists of three books: *Inferno, Purgatorio,* and *Paradiso.* It is, in fact, an autobiographical work describing his spiritual journey.

Comment: A famous psychologist said: "If you want to insure your future, get rid of your past."

Dr. Hora: What does it mean to insure the future?

Comment: I guess he was talking about improving experiences which are to come.

Dr. Hora: That's what psychoanalysis is attempting to accomplish; it tries to help people to improve their experiences by sort of undoing the past.

Comment: Didn't you say that one can have as many experiences as one wants as long as one is not interested in them?

Dr. Hora: Yes, that's a good position to take in regard to experiences. Of course, experiences are inevitable but not necessary. So if we go for a vacation or to a fancy restaurant or to a party, the best way to participate is with little interest.

Comment: We are only interested in the good of God.

Dr. Hora: Right. The first commandment implies: "Thou shalt have no other interests before the good of God." Most of the time we are suffering from what we are interested in. Whatever we are interested in becomes a "should," and it is the "should" thoughts which are our tormentors. "Should-lessness" is freedom and peace. Life ceases to be a hassle.

Comment: This is wonderful and it is true, no matter what anybody says; and yet, as soon as I get into my work environment I seem to lose it.

Comment: I was going to say the same thing. While I sit here, this wonderful idea is so simple, I get all enthusiastic about it, I look forward to going home and living accordingly. But then my interest must change because my resolve falls apart. What happens there?

Dr. Hora: You are describing what appears to be an acceptance of the principle but not a commitment to the principle. It is easy to accept something that is so logical and clear, but the next step is commitment. "Commit thy works unto the Lord, and thy thoughts shall be established" (Proverbs 16:3).

Question: Well, what do you mean by commitment? Dedication?

Dr. Hora: It is a sincere desire to apply the principle every moment of our day, to live by it. If you don't use it, you lose it.

Question: What helps us to be steadfast in our commitment to this principle?

Dr. Hora: Suffering or wisdom. The sufferer is driven to it, and the wise man is drawn to it.

Comment: The paradox is that if you commit yourself to this principle, your experiences tend to improve.

Comment: It seems that what we need is a mental gatekeeper who would control and choose the thoughts which come into our consciousness and remind us whether they are important or unimportant. Is there such a gatekeeper? And if there is one, who is it, or what is it?

Dr. Hora: The gatekeeper is the truth in consciousness. For instance, if we didn't know that two and two is four, we would never notice a mathematical error, we would be completely unaware that there is an error in a computation. Therefore, it is not really we who are correcting an error but the truth in consciousness. The truth is the mathematician and the truth of the first commandment is the gatekeeper.

The more clearly we understand the truth of God and man, and the more clearly it is established in our consciousness what is existentially valid, the more alert the gatekeeper becomes. The gatekeeper is not a person, nor is it mind, it is the truth itself. If the truth is not clearly established in consciousness, then we are lacking an effective gatekeeper; all sorts of suggestions and invalid ideas can sneak in and result in experiences. Therefore, it is urgent that the truth be clearly established in consciousness. When Adam and Eve were expelled from paradise, God established cherubim with flaming swords to guard against their reentrance. That's the gatekeeper guarding the paradise of spiritual consciousness. Sometimes garbage thoughts come to us with a promise of heavenly experiences, they knock on our doors and promise heavenly pleasures and experiences and if the gatekeeper is not very alert, he lets them in. Sometimes the gatekeeper is overwhelmed by intimidation, provocation, or seduction.

Comment: This is really a wonderful metaphor—this gatekeeper idea.

Dr. Hora: We have to come to realize that no good is good but the good God gives. There are many things that masquerade as good and knock on our door for acceptance. But if we understand the true nature of good, then it is easy to look at those counterfeit goods with a sort of detachment, with not much interest. And so we can go everywhere and do everything other people do, but with not too much interest.

Comment: But with enthusiasm.

Dr. Hora: Yes, because enthusiasm means to be with God, and God is our primary interest.

Dialogue No. 31

MEEKNESS AND HUMILITY

Question: Could we talk some more about meekness and humility? What are they and how could we become meek and humble?

Dr. Hora: Humility and meekness are the most precious qualities than man can acquire.

Comment: That would suggest that man isn't born humble.

Dr. Hora: No, he isn't. Man is born ignorant, and he gets worse as time goes by.

Comment: He becomes more and more miseducated.

Dr. Hora: Right. What is the great value of humility? It is very simple: meekness and humility make life easy. It is the secret of the harmonious, trouble-free, effortless life. Jesus said: "Learn of me; for I am meek and lowly in heart: and ye shall find rest unto your souls. For my yoke is easy, and my burden is light" (Matthew 11: 29,30). So, in juxtaposition to this, whenever we feel like complaining about how hard life is, how heavy a burden we have to carry, how nothing seems to be working out, how people maltreat us, how complicated everything is becoming in life, we can ask instead: "What is the meaning of this?" Perhaps it is a sign that we are not sufficiently "shouldless" and not sufficiently humble.

Question: When we see a child manifesting the error of willfulness, how do we apply this knowledge so that he should become "shouldless"?

Dr. Hora: We are not saying that people should become "shouldless." We only say that it is good to be "shouldless." We absolutely respect people's freedom and right to be wrong. By the way, let us understand that "shouldlessness" is synonymous with meekness. The Bible says: "Blessed are the meek: for they shall inherit the earth" (Matthew 5:5). In our terms it means: Blessed are the shouldless: for their lives shall be uncomplicated (fussless).

Comment: Children seem to incite in us "should" reactions.

Dr. Hora: One thing must be clearly understood, namely, that "should" thinking does not come from the children spontaneously; the thinking of children is the expression of the mental climate in the home. If the mental climate in the home is a "shouldless" one, then the children will not be willful. And if the mental climate is a willful one, then the children will, of course, manifest it. And the same is true of humility. If the mental climate in the home is a spiritual one, the children will be naturally humble. We cannot blame the children for eliciting willfulness in us. Whatever the quality of our perspective is will determine the climate in the home, and everyone in it will be effected. It is, of course, much easier to become willful than humble, it is much easier to become arrogant than meek. We seem to learn the wrong things faster.

Question: What is the role of intellectual vanity in connection with attaining humility? Is there something special required to heal intellectual vanity?

Dr. Hora: Yes, intellectual vanity is very difficult to heal because if we are intellectually vain, we are too embarrassed to accept a healing.

Comment: That sounds almost hopeless.

Dr. Hora: Yes. But, of course, there comes a time when intellectual vanity becomes so painful and expensive that one reaches a crisis, and will say: "Enough is enough, I just have to accept a healing no matter how humiliating it is."

Question: What is intellectual vanity?

Dr. Hora: It is a desire to be admired for how clever we are. It is a desire for admiration of our minds.

Comment: It is a plague. I experienced quite often the difficulty of accepting a healing, so I know well what you are talking about. Sometimes I come to the point where I see that all that is needed is one little step to be healed, but I cling to my image of myself.

Dr. Hora: A psychiatrist told me a story about a woman who came to see him. When she entered the office, she looked him over from head to toe and said: "And you take it into your head that you can help me?"

Question: What is the most important thing to know in order to be healed of intellectual vanity?

Dr. Hora: That God is the only Mind.

Comment: But it is vanity that stops one from accepting that. So then where are we?

Dr. Hora: Then we have a choice of two things: the way of suffering or the way of wisdom.

Question: Will vanity fall away from lack of interest at some point?

Dr. Hora: Yes, it falls away from pain.

Comment: I would like to go back to the issue of humility and meekness. Sometimes I go from arrogance and willfulness to complete surrender to another and become a doormat. Whenever I hear the word "meekness," I immediately see myself in a situation where I am letting people step all over me.

Dr. Hora: Recently, a congressman made a speech, and he started out by saying: "I am humbly proud." This illustrates the problem which we could call the perversity of the human mind. If we try to be humble in terms of relationships with people, it will never work. Humility and meekness are not human qualities. They are not something that we can cultivate as a technique of getting along with people; they are strictly spiritual qualities, and they refer to our understanding of our relationship with God. Humility and meekness are not psychological but spiritual.

What you just described was an illustration of the pitfall of horizontal thinking. Psychology and psychoanalysis are absolutely incapable of ever helping people attain true humility and meekness because, in the human sphere of reasoning, it is not possible to be humble without being proud that one is humble. We have these ridiculous dualisms of yes and no, and no and yes. It is only through God that true meekness and humility are realized. And that meekness, that humility, is not proud; it is dignified, inspired, intelligent, peaceful, assured, alert, responsive, and highly effective. It is not a form of behavior but, rather, a quality of consciousness.

Question: How can God become real to us?

Dr. Hora: In the case of intellectual vanity we must reach a point where we are willing to be embarrassed, and that usually comes when we are at the end of our rope. Vain people are awfully resistant to embarrassment; they consider it the worst thing that could happen to them. And yet, until we are willing to be embarrassed, nothing will happen. To a vain individual, it is highly embarrassing to accept a healing because everything then collapses. But in the embarrassment there is the possibility of healing.

Question: What makes embarrassment so embarrassing?

Dr. Hora: Well, the vain individual finds it difficult to admit that he is not smart enough to handle his problems.

Comment: It is quite embarrassing to seek help from a psychiatrist, but to seek help from God seems even more embarrassing.

Question: Would you, please, explain again what humility is. Is it "shouldlessness"?

Dr. Hora: "Shouldlessness" is meekness. Humility was explained by Jesus when he said: "I can of mine own self do nothing" (John 5:30). And: ". . . the Father that dwelleth in me, he doeth the works" (John 14:10). Sometimes it is very hard for us to admit that we cannot cure ourselves, or that we cannot solve our problems.

Comment: But if you are going to a psychiatrist regularly, you are obviously admitting that you cannot handle your problems.

Dr. Hora: That's just it; you are going there to learn how to handle your problems by yourself. Yesterday I spoke to a young man who told me that he traveled all over the world seeking to be healed of his problem, and no one could help him. So I asked him: "Were you looking to be healed or were you seeking to learn the technique of curing yourself?" When we are looking to find out how to heal ourselves, we can never be healed. We can only get healed if God heals us; not a psychiatrist or anyone else or we ourselves, but God. "I am the Lord that healeth thee" (Exodus 15:26). ". . . Who healeth all thy diseases; who redeemeth thy life from destruction" (Psalms 103: 3,4).

Comment: I thought that my knowing God would heal me.

Dr. Hora: Your knowing how to *let* God heal you will heal you. God helps those who let him. Vanity is too proud to let God help. If, however, we take the path of wisdom, practice listening to what God says, and put aside personal opinions, calculative thinking, and the tendency to outline what should be or what shouldn't be, then we shall fulfill the biblical recommendation: "Trust in the Lord with all thine heart; and lean not unto thine own understanding. In all thy ways acknowledge him, and he shall direct thy paths" (Proverbs 3: 5, 6).

Dialogue No. 32

IS GOD SLOW?

Dr. Hora: Sometimes we have the impression that God is very slow in responding to our prayers. What could be the meaning of that?

Comment: I usually blame myself for not asking the right questions or thinking the right thoughts in order to bring about the goodness of God.

Dr. Hora: Is God slow?

Comment: How could he be slow if he is right there in everything? It is our own understanding of the "isness" of God that is lacking.

Question: Isn't it also a question of sincerity?

Dr. Hora: Could you explain that?

Comment: It seems to me that if I need help, I must be sincere in turning to God.

Comment: I heard a story about some people who set sail on a nice, windy day; they were sailing for hours without increasing their distance from the shore. They forgot to pull up the anchor.

Dr. Hora: This is a very good analogy. What does the anchor stand for in terms of our theme?

Comment: Our problems, ideas, and hang-ups; whatever we are cherishing.

Comment: Ignorance is the anchor.

Dr. Hora: Let us remember now that we are trying to understand the meaning of God's seeming slowness in coming to our rescue. Essentially, the problem is the tendency to pray for the solution of our problems. This seems very justified and rational; however, it is futile.

Comment: Because we are making the problem a reality and giving it power.

Comment: We are not looking for the meaning of the problem.

Comment: We must look for the dissolution of the problem rather than for the solution.

Comment: There is some quality of God which we need to realize.

Dr. Hora: Suppose someone has a splitting headache?

Comment: The fact is that we cannot ask God to solve our problems because he doesn't know anything about problems.

Dr. Hora: Then what's the sense of praying?

Comment: We pray in order to get into harmony with God.

Dr. Hora: This is very strange, indeed. Here we are faced with a problem and we are not supposed to pray for the solution of that problem. As long as we are involved with the problem and desire to be relieved of it, we are anchored in that problem. For instance, when we have a headache, all we can think of is how to get rid of this headache.

Comment: So we are involved with materialism instead of with God, which is spirit.

Question: What if you pray to see God?

Dr. Hora: If we are blessed enough to discern the meaning of a symptom—for instance, in the case of a headache—we may become aware of resentfulness. Then, of course, we can turn our attention to the fact that God is love—all-forgiving, infinitely merciful, joyous, harmonious love—and we focus our thoughts on this fact and seek to completely involve ourselves with this thought. At that moment the headache is gone.

Comment: Because the seeing is the healing of the resentment.

Dr. Hora: Right. God seems slow in coming to our aid if we are slow in turning away from our problems, which is the anchor. All problems are distractions from the one overriding necessity of seeing God ever more clearly, and to find our peace in him. Saint Augustine said: "Thou hast made us for thyself, and our hearts are restless until we find our peace in thee." The solution to every problem, whether physical, emotional, financial, personal, or collective, is to find our peace in God, to see our at-one-ment with divine reality.

Comment: I had an interesting dream. I saw a glass container filled with very ugly insects and I felt revulsion in looking at them. But then the thought occurred to me, God has never made anything ugly and evil, and at that moment the insects disappeared.

Dr. Hora: God is omnipresent, and sometimes we experience instantaneous healings even of the most complicated problems.

Question: But what if the problem is more complicated than a headache, and is accompanied by a great deal of fear?

Dr. Hora: As an experienced yachtsman you realize that there are more elaborate anchors. But essentially, they all have to be pulled up if we want the boat to get going. And with our problems it is analogous; no matter how complex, we must find a way of letting go of them. How would you go about losing your briefcase, for instance?

Comment: I guess I would have to become interested in something else very intently.

Dr. Hora: Yes, we have to turn our attention so wholeheartedly to God, to divine reality, that we completely lose awareness of the problem—and that's the healing.

Most of our problems indicate that we are seeing ourselves apart from God, in some kind of different context; either completely autonomous or in a family context, a group context, a professional context, a social context, or in a national or international context. The smaller the context in which we see ourselves as existing, the sicker we are. What is the smallest context in which we can see ourselves?

Comment: It is the physical self.

Dr. Hora: Right.

Comment: And God is the largest and widest context.

Dr. Hora: Yes, God is the context of infinity. Reality is unlimited; therefore, all contexts which are smaller than infinity are, by definition, invalid. In order to be healthy we have to live in reality, and reality is infinite Love-Intelligence, God. The more clearly we are able to see ourselves as existing in the context of infinity, the healthier we are.

Question: What about doing preparatory work, let us say for teaching? I find myself most reluctant to do it. It has always been a problem to me.

Dr. Hora: What is the best way to prepare for a class or a business conference or any endeavor? The best way is to go into meditation, become very quiet, and endeavor to establish a clear consciousness of our total at-one-ment with infinite Mind, God, Love-Intelligence. That is the best way to prepare for any activity. When we are able to see ourselves as living in the context of infinite Mind, which is the "secret place of the most High," we will be able observe God in action. "My Father worketh hitherto, and I work" (John 5:17). The Bible says: "Draw nigh to God, and he will draw nigh to you" (James 4:8). It would be helpful to ask ourselves frequently: "In what context are our thoughts revolving most of the time?"

Question: What would you say is the context of someone who is mostly concerned with feeling good?

Dr. Hora: That's the narrowest possible context of self-indulgent narcissism. Jesus said: "I am come that they might have life, and that they might have it more abundantly" (John 10:10). What did he mean?

Comment: By enlarging the context of our existence into infinity, all good comes to us through God.

Comment: I have always lived in the context of my relationship to my mother and actually identified myself with her. But now I am trying to break out of this imprisoning context by realizing that God is my mother.

Comment: I felt the very same thing when it became clear to me that my parents were not my parents and that God was my father and my mother. From that point on everything changed. It was a tremendously liberating experience to be a child of God rather than a child of people who, naturally, were not very enlightened.

Dialogue No. 33

ANXIETY

Question: Could we talk about anxiety?

Dr. Hora: All right. What is anxiety? What does it mean when we are anxious?

Comment: Is anxiety the worry that one will not be able to fulfill one's desires?

Dr. Hora: Anxiety is anxiety, and worry is worry. Anxiety is anxiousness. And what is anxiousness? The English word is self-explanatory. Anxiousness means that we want something. For instance, we are anxious to go on a vacation; we are anxious to make progress; we are anxious to succeed. Anxiety is a thought of what should be. Worry is a thought of what should not be.

Comment: Anxiety can also be looked upon as a sign indicating to us that we are on the wrong track.

Dr. Hora: Yes. Anxiety is often inevitable, but it is not necessary. Is it possible to live in such a way as to be free of wanting things?

Comment: Yes, but it is not normal. According to psychologists, it is normal to be anxious.

Dr. Hora: Probably nowhere in the world are there so many anxious people as in the United States, and nowhere in the world are so many tranquilizers consumed as in the United States. This is the price of freedom of opportunity and possibilities for social and economic advancement. Our wants are constantly being stimulated by the news media, which create a psychology of rising expectations and infinite consumer appetites. Our culture encourages ambition and competition, and we are constantly being stimulated to want things. The more intensely we want something, the more anxious we become.

Question: Where does freedom come in here?

Dr. Hora: Our culture interprets freedom as license. The freedom of upward mobility creates anxiety; and if we fail to achieve our objectives, we suffer a sense of defeat, shame, depression, and even bitterness. We may even become hostile or despairing, which, in turn, can lead to illnesses of various sorts.

Since being anxious is clearly troublesome, we must acknowledge that ambition is existentially invalid, in spite of the fact that our culture approves of it and fosters it. Ambition disturbs the harmony of individual existence, family life, and community conditions. If we are ambitious, every fellow human being becomes, more or less, an enemy because he stands in our way. Husbands and wives can get caught up in rivalry with each other, especially now with the emphasis on women's liberation. Marriages are under great stress; instead of harmony and mutual support, there is competition between husbands and wives. They are concerned about whose career is more important, who can earn more money, who is more famous or more powerful, who is getting ahead faster. This has a disruptive effect on families; the children are contaminated by this kind of thinking and become disturbed and overactive. The question could be asked: "What then is a healthy alternative to ambition and to wanting and not wanting, for it is not good to want and it is not good not to want?"

Comment: The important thing is to want the right things, and to know what is really good.

Dr. Hora: Now what will happen to anxiety when we want something that is really good? Suppose we want enlightenment? We must be very careful because it is possible to want the right thing the wrong way. Occasionally it happens when we are on the spiritual path that we become very ambitious about reaching enlightenment, and then we have a problem where we want the right thing but we want it the wrong way. In the Bible this is referred to as "spiritual wickedness." Ambition can be a sneaky problem, it can contaminate even the purest of aspirations, and we must guard against that. What is required of us is alertness and discipline of mind; and every time an ambitious thought occurs, we must quickly repudiate it, dismiss it, and replace it with a right thought.

Question: What is a right thought?

Dr. Hora: A right thought always starts with God as the source of all good. Then there will be no anxiety, no excitement, no frustration, and no depression. What will there be?

Comment: Peace, assurance, gratitude, love.

Dr. Hora: There will be existential fulfillment, which is based on the realization that God expresses himself through man as Love-Intelligence.

Dialogue No. 34

BELIEVING AND KNOWING

Question: Is it true that what is real to you is what you believe? If you believe that evil is real, then it is real to you. And if you believe that God has nothing to do with evil, that God is real and good is real, then does that determine your experiences? It seems to me that one is no more absolutely real than the other; it all depends on what you choose. And Jesus came along and said: This is the way to be happy; you just believe that God is good and God is real, and then you will experience good whether there is such a thing or not.

Comment: It occurred to me that some experiences are therapeutic—like, for instance, spirituality—but I think that's not just an idea, that's a fact.

Dr. Hora: Jesus didn't say: Ye shall believe in the right things, and the belief in the right things will make you free. He said: "Ye shall know the truth, and the truth shall make you free" (John 8:32). Certainly, our beliefs determine our experiences. Now the question is, what happens if we believe in the truth?

Comment: We wind up getting involved in contentious arguments and polemics.

Dr. Hora: Yes, we become religious dogmaticists and live in fear of someone perhaps succeeding in throwing a monkey wrench into our belief system. Believers are very vulnerable. This is the basis of religious intolerance through the ages. As long as people are believing in something, whether it is valid or invalid, they are in the position of believers, and that is precarious. Someone may come along and shake their faith, and then they get confused. Some people even become violent out of the fear that their belief systems will be proven invalid. If we believe in something, we are ideological or emotional about it; we can believe in something with our intellect or with our emotions. If we believe with our emotions, we can become emotionally disturbed; if we believe intellectually, we may tend to become argumentative. The history of religious intolerance and warfare is rooted in the fact that people were led to believe rather than to understand. It is, of course, easy to become a believer. We just join a group, an organization, a movement, or a church, and we participate in a collective belief. As long as no one is challenging our beliefs, we are comfortable. This is the explanation of group formations. All over the world people have a tendency to join organizations and clubs. There is a certain comfort in knowing that others believe what we believe.

Comment: Safety in numbers?

Dr. Hora: Right. However, we do not believe in believing, because belief prevents us from coming to know. Someone may say at this point that the Bible is full of exhortations to believe, and that even Jesus spoke of the need to believe. However, epistemological and linguistic studies give us sufficient justification to reinterpret the word "believing" as connoting more a need to understand. Therefore, wherever the word "believe" appears in the Bible, it seems more profitable to substitute the word "understand."

Interestingly enough, it is impossible to understand something that is not true; for instance, it is impossible to understand that two and two is five. It can only be believed. It is possible to believe that two and two is four, but it is much better to understand it.

Question: How do we know whether we are believing something or understanding it?

Dr. Hora: In the light of what was just said, how do we know?

Comment: Belief would always be accompanied by a sense of uncertainty and doubt; with understanding there is a sense of assurance and clarity.

Comment: But one can deceive oneself.

Dr. Hora: Right. Furthermore, believing tends to result in experiences; understanding leads to realizations.

Comment: When we appreciate the difference between realizations and experiences, we lose interest in experiencing and enjoy the peace and freedom of right knowing.

Dr. Hora: Interestingly enough, there is a large quantity of literature speaking of religious experiences. One of the most famous of these is a book by William James entitled *Varieties of Religious Experience.* If we come to understand the truth of being, it will not result in religious experience but in enlightenment, which is not an experience but a realization. Jesus recommended that we aim at coming to know the truth, and that it will make us free. Free from what?

Comment: From the problems of believing.

Dr. Hora: Once we understand divine life, God, we will never have to believe anything at all, and that is a great freedom.

Comment: It just occurred to me that when we believe something we are forced to convince ourselves again and again that what we believe is true, and that's what we are doing when we keep reconfirming our egos.

Dr. Hora: What do we call that?

Comment: Self-confirmatory ideation.

Dr. Hora: When we are believers, we are doubters. It is impossible to be a believer without being a doubter at the same time, because if we didn't doubt, we wouldn't have to believe; this explains the dynamism of insecurity. When we come to know the truth and understand God in an existentially valid way, we are liberated from the necessity to believe anything. Carl Jung was once asked the question whether he believed in God, and he said: "I don't have to believe, I know."

Understanding is a higher level of consciousness, it cannot be willed, it can only be sought. It is important to know the difference between willing something and seeking something.

Comment: The difference is humility.

Dr. Hora: The Bible says: "If thou seek him, he will be found of thee" (I Chronicles 28:9). "If ye seek him, he will be found of you" (II Chronicles 15:2). "And ye shall seek me, and find me, when ye shall search for me with all your heart" (Jeremiah 29:13).

Dialogue No. 35

INDESTRUCTIBLE LIFE

Question: How do we know that we are children of God?

Dr. Hora: Well, that is an interesting question.

Question: What is man?

Dr. Hora: That is an even better question. Man is what God has created; man is a creation of God.

Question: Isn't man an illusion?

Dr. Hora: What do you mean?

Comment: How could God have created man if man is an illusion?

Dr. Hora: Who said man is an illusion? What kind of man did God create?

Comment: In the image and likeness of himself, according to the Bible.

Dr. Hora: Instead of just believing the literal meaning of words, let us try to understand. What does it mean to be an image and likeness of God?

Question: To be an expression of God?

Dr. Hora: Jesus said: "He that hath seen me hath seen the Father" (John 14:9). What was he saying?

Comment: Insofar as man is an image and likeness of God, he is inconceivable, intangible, invisible, yet knowable, just as God is.

Dr. Hora: Right. No one has ever seen the real man; the real man cannot be seen, just as God cannot be seen. But goodness and love, intelligence, beauty, joy, harmony, power, and wisdom can be seen—not with the eyes but by spiritual discernment. We all have a special faculty to see the invisible, and we have to cultivate it. In some people this faculty is highly developed. Who are these people? Artists and beholders, or so-called spiritual seers. What is an artist? An artist is not someone who paints pictures—anyone can paint pictures.

What makes an artist? In what way is an artist different from other people? He has a more developed faculty of aesthetic perceptivity. And what is an enlightened man?

Comment: He is someone with a highly developed faculty of spiritual perception.

Dr. Hora: Right. And what is a musician and what is a composer? There are musicians and there are composers, not every musician is a composer. Arthur Rubinstein always speaks with great admiration about composers, he himself is only a brilliant musician. A composer expresses creativity; a musician is an interpreter of what has been created. What does a composer create? He hears silent sounds.

Comment: You can hear music in your head.

Dr. Hora: We can hear music in our soul. Beethoven was deaf, and still he was able to compose symphonies. In his consciousness he could envision a complete symphony and write it down. That is an example of beholding something that is not material; it is intangible, unimaginable. He could conceive the inconceivable. Man has great potentialities which go unrecognized under ordinary circumstances. The ability of envisioning is synonymous with beholding and is a God-given faculty. The fact that we do have this faculty is additional proof that we are spiritual.

A very unenlightened individual has a very limited awareness of reality Most of his awareness is absorbed in feelings and sensations; he is inclined to be concretistic. He thinks in concrete terms. On a somewhat higher level, man has the faculty of abstract thinking; he is aware of ideas and appreciates them. An artist has expanded his ability to see into spheres of aesthetic appreciation, which is neither concrete nor abstract. He can perceive beauty, harmony, color, form, order, joy, love, and meaning. The supreme faculty is the enlightened man's ability to behold reality, which is spiritual, suprasensory, transcendent. Then he can find God manifesting himself as man. So the supreme attainment for man is to be a beholder, a fully conscious manifestation of God's being.

Question: Does it require a special gift?

Dr. Hora: Yes and no. First of all, everyone must, sooner or later, become a beholder; the entire human race has to eventually become beholders; this is the portent of evolution. There are individuals who are the cutting edge of the evolutionary process. Jesus was spearheading this process; he was and is thousands of years in advance of the rest of us in the fullness of his ability to behold. Throughout history and in the present time there are more and more individuals who are in the forefront of the evolutionary process in their faculty to behold, and these are called avatars or prophets or models of spiritual excellence.

Question: How can we be protected from becoming smug and secretly proud of ourselves for being on the spiritual path?

Dr. Hora: Anyone who would be tempted to think this way would clearly show his ignorance and lack of understanding. For anyone, even those with only a little understanding, must be mindful of what Jesus said about himself: "I am among you as he that serveth" (Luke 22:27). He was light years ahead of his fellow men and yet he did not consider himself superior but rather a servant. The more we can behold divine reality, the more humble, loving, and patient we become. We have an increasing desire to be beneficial presences in the world; the idea of becoming members of a spiritual elite would be abhorrent.

Comment: But life can be lived on many levels. When I watch television I am keenly aware of this, and I am also aware of living on a superior level.

Dr. Hora: The spiritual is not superior, it is just more real. There is no hierarchy of values between the spiritual and material, there is just reality and illusion. Illusion is very painful and difficult, full of trouble. Reality is harmonious and all good, frictionless. Jesus said: "In the world ye shall have tribulation: but be of good cheer; I have overcome the world" (John 16:33).

Comment: For a long time I thought that an artist would try to overcome the world with aesthetic values, but then I realized that this cannot be done, that it takes a total spiritual enlightenment to overcome the world, that the aesthetic values which an artist expresses are more of a symbolic means pointing to something else. The appreciation of beauty is only one step on the way.

Dr. Hora: Right. Otherwise all artists would be enlightened.

Comment: And they are not.

Dr. Hora: What happens when an artist becomes enlightened?

Comment: He is no longer an artist.

Dr. Hora: Right. He becomes a beholder. Life itself becomes a work of art; his focus is on being. Jesus never painted a picture, never wrote a book; he didn't even write down the Sermon on the Mount. All his talents were channeled into actualizing a perfect life. His medium of artistic expression was himself. He said: "I am the way, the truth, and the life" (John 14:6). An artist says: Look at this picture and you will see beauty and a certain quality of awareness. Jesus said: Look at me and you will see God, perfect being, truth. He was an artist, wasn't he? His greatest work of art was the crucifixion. Isn't this a shocking thing to say? What was he doing when he had himself crucified? He was saying: Divine life is indestructible, you cannot kill it. You can crucify the body, but life goes on. Isn't this a supreme work of art?

Comment: But Dr. Hora, the violence that is expressed in the crucifixion is difficult for me to accept, since Jesus was a man of peace and had no interest in violence. I cannot reconcile the idea of peace and beauty and harmony and love with his violent death, since we do invite what happens to us.

Dr. Hora: As I just explained, Jesus was demonstrating to the world that life cannot be destroyed. So he allowed the body to be killed, and then he came out of the tomb alive. He wanted to demonstrate to the world that life is not synonymous with the body. "I am the resurrection, and the life: he that believeth in me, though he were dead, yet shall he live" (John 11:25).

Comment: I was wondering whether maybe we all have to undergo some sort of crucifixion experiences in life before we can understand what he was demonstrating. Is that so?

Dr. Hora: One could intepret physical sufferings as analogies to the crucifixion, or the pain of giving up ego gratifications. Jesus' intention was that we would learn from his demonstration so that we would be spared sufferings ourselves. But people misunderstood and became fascinated with the idea of violence. The issue of violence has nothing to do with it. The issue of indestructible life is the point of the crucifixion. When we see it that way we can see that it was a tremendous demonstration on his part, that he was a teacher of immense magnitude.

Comment: It seems that dying daily to our personal sense is our crucifixion.

Dr. Hora: You notice how you are again gravitating toward thinking of the crucifixion in the context of suffering. The issue of the crucifixion is not suffering but triumph. Jesus was not interested in suffering, and some believe he wasn't suffering at all. Nobody can understand the crucifixion as long as he is thinking of it primarily in terms of suffering. The demonstration of indestructible life is the meaning of the crucifixion.

Dialogue No. 36

SELF-CONFIRMATORY
IDEATION

Question: On previous occasions you pointed out the importance of three factors in our experience: what we cherish, what we hate, and what we fear. Isn't it true that they are all the same?

Dr. Hora: What you are saying is that there must be a common denominator in these three factors.

Comment: The common denominator must be that they indicate the worshiping of something other than God.

Dr. Hora: Right. The common denominator is that they all have a self-confirmatory quality.

Comment: Fear seems to be somewhat different. What is it that we fear? What is fear? Is it that our life is threatened?

Dr. Hora: You are confusing two questions. You are asking: "What is fear?" And you are also asking: "What are we afraid of?" But mostly you are asking: "What are we afraid of?" If we ask "What am I afraid of?" then we have already accepted the reality of fear; we have accepted that fear has an object. If fear has an object, then it seems to be real and justified. It is therefore futile to ask what we are afraid of.

Question: Is it like asking what's wrong?

Dr. Hora: Yes. The right question to ask is: "What is fear?" Fear is self-confirmatory mental preoccupation; it says: "I am" afraid. What is pain?

Comment: Pain says: "I am" suffering.

Dr. Hora: We are always running into trouble when we ask wrong questions. If we ask a right question there is always an answer—and the answer can be helpful. The question now is: "How can we be healed of self-confirmatory ideation?" Every form of self-confirmatory ideation is a false claim which says "I am," and there is no such thing. The Bible says God is the only "I am." This was the first lesson God taught Moses: "I am the only I am, beside me there is none else." Therefore, it is a mistake for anyone to entertain thoughts starting with "I am." Man is a manifestation of God's being; he does not have an "I am" of his own—it just seems that way. Once we understand that, then there is no fear, fear is not possible; God is never afraid.

Comment: These things become clearer to us when we learn to replace self-confirmatory ideation with God-confirmatory ideation. Thursday I came in here with a great sense of fear about what seemed to be a medical problem. But very quickly it became clear that "I am" was the only issue. Oddly enough, we didn't dwell much on the symptoms, or what was going to be done about it. We just tried to see that this "I am" was false and that the remedy was God-confirmatory ideation. By focusing on existentially valid issues, my fear was dispelled, and my problem turned out to be trivial.

Dr. Hora: It is helpful to learn the fact that when we see each other, we are seeing individual manifestations of the great "I AM." We must transcend personalities and seemingly self-existent organisms. Every life form is a manifestation of the God Principle. If we learn to see life this way, we will find that our outlook is transformed, and we become fearless and loving.

Comment: Last weekend I took my two cats to the country. While I was out, a marauding tomcat came in and apparently frightened them. One of them ran away and hasn't come back. Of course, I worried and didn't know what to do, and I feel very responsible and guilty. I hope to keep on looking for her next weekend.

Comment: Once you said to us that loss is gain. How does it apply here?

Dr. Hora: If we can learn something useful from this seeming loss, then it can be a gain. What we are seeing is an exaggerated sense of personal responsibility, self-blame, crying—which is self-pity—fear, guilt, sorrow, befuddlement, and the asking of futile questions. As you see, it will not facilitate the finding or survival of the cat if there is self-confirmatory ideation. Our problems are always tailor-made, and they come to us for our edification. What is the lesson that needs to be learned from this problem? Who is the keeper of the cat? The Bible says: "The Lord is thy keeper: the Lord is thy shade upon thy right hand. The sun shall not smite thee by day, nor the moon by night. The Lord shall preserve thee from all evil: he shall preserve thy soul. The Lord shall preserve thy going out and thy coming in from this time forth, and even for evermore" (Psalms 121:5–8). In other words, when we are tempted to engage in self-confirmatory ideation, we must quickly turn to God-confirmatory ideation. If we do this, we can always expect some favorable resolution of whatever problem we may be facing. Can anyone explain how this is possible?

Comment: It is possible because the essence of our problems is always self-confirmatory ideation.

Dr. Hora: Right. Is this understood by all? Let us try to illustrate this point. When we are faced with a problem like this one, for instance, we usually start thinking: my problem is that the cat ran away, and the other problem is how to get her back. This may be the issue, but it is not the problem. The problem is always self-confirmatory thinking, which consists of a belief in personal ownership, attachment, cherishing a possession, having a false sense of responsibility, seeking to blame, and asking what to do about it and how to do it. We must understand that God is perfect reality, so perfect that nothing can be put to it nor taken away from it. And to be on the spiritual path means learning to see the divine perfection which is present right where the troubles of the world seem to be.

However, someone may ask: "Isn't this just Pollyanna thinking, or wishful thinking?" Or someone may ask: "Isn't it too good or too easy to be true?"

Comment: What needs to be seen is that thought and experience are related.

Dr. Hora: Suppose, with the case of the missing cat, we were to ask: "Who is to blame for it?"

Comment: But that's an invalid question.

Dr. Hora: Do you really understand that? What makes it

invalid is that as long as we entertain this question in thought, our prayers are futile, ineffective.

Comment: If we are blaming, then we are believing in a power apart from God.

Dr. Hora: Do you all know the story of the blind boy whom Jesus healed? People were asking him: "Who is to blame for that boy's condition?" And he said: "No one is to blame. This is an opportunity to discern the glory, power, and love of God." Similarly, the owner of this cat needs to learn how to overcome self-confirmatory ideation. And this is the secret lesson which is built into the problem.

Dialogue No. 37

POWER STRUGGLE

Question: How could one be healed of the tendency to get involved in power struggles?

Dr. Hora: This is a very common experience. One of the most typical and childish forms of it can be seen in what is called "Indian wrestling." But Indian wrestling can go on in many forms and on many levels of human interaction.

Comment: It is a phenomenon of two egos claiming power.

Dr. Hora: Yes, two nonexistent egos claiming nonexistent powers.

Comment: I usually submit.

Dr. Hora: Is submitting the solution to power struggle?

Comment: I know it isn't, but that's how I handle it.

Comment: The best way to deal with it is to refuse to see life as the other sees it.

Comment: When people are involved in a power struggle, it seems that the world is not big enough for both of them.

Dr. Hora: There is one helpful point relevant to this problem: we can abolish the thought of wanting and not wanting.

Question: But what takes its place?

Dr. Hora: Is. *Is* is the greatest word ever uttered; this small word is the greatest in our language.

Question: How about "I don't care"? Or is that a cop-out?

Dr. Hora: Yes, that is a cop-out; it is just a self-deception. "I don't care" leads to apathy and depression, defeatism and secret vindictiveness, which brings us back into the power struggle. In the realm of Love-Intelligence there is neither self nor other, there is only that which *is.*

Question: What is man's idea of power?

Dr. Hora: Getting what we want and imposing our will on others.

Question: What is apathy?

Dr. Hora: Apathy is a pretense of resignation and an acceptance of defeat. But it is not a passive condition because underneath there is a strong vindictive desire. So the power struggle continues even after seeming acceptance of defeat. Giving in, therefore, is not a solution. The whole philosophy of passive resistance—as advocated by Gandhi, the Quakers, Martin Luther King—is just a passive way of participating in a power struggle.

Comment: If only one could have a way of knowing that God really is, then one could be healed of this problem. Is there a sign which could provide us with some evidence of God's power and presence?

Dr. Hora: Yes, there is. It is a subjective sign and we have called it PAGL—peace, assurance, gratitude, and love. This sign gives a subjective sense of being in harmony with God and that, regardless of the human situation, all is well.

Let us consider the state of consciousness in which people experience a power struggle. There is tension, anxiety, resentment, restlessness, vindictiveness, unhappiness; the mind is racing, agitated. All this is the opposite of PAGL, which is a spiritual sign that makes it possible for us to be aware of God's presence and reality. This way God is not a mystery and we are not dependent on miracles. Jesus said: "Except ye see signs and wonders, ye will not believe" (John 4:48).

If we cultivate an appreciation of spiritual values and an understanding of spiritual good, of which PAGL is an indicator, we shall be spared getting hooked on many wants and don't wants. We shall then be spared the developing of false appetites. We will be protected from all the enticements and ambitions of materialism which lead to power struggles.

Question: What is grace?

Dr. Hora: The Bible says: "My grace is sufficient for thee" (II Corinthians 12:9). Grace is the synonym for spiritual good. If we appreciate the good of God, which is spiritual, we are living in grace, and that provides for all our needs. God's grace and God's love are freely available to all who are interested in them. We don't have to deserve it; God is not a merit system. "The publicans and the sinner go into the kingdom

before the Pharisees." How is that possible? What kind of justice is that? In a merit system this would make no sense.
Comment: That's why grace is spoken of as a "free gift."
Dr. Hora: The right understanding of and reliance on grace lifts us out of the seeming necessity for engaging in power struggles.

Dialogue No. 38

WHAT IS HYPNOTISM?

Question: What is hypnotism?

Comment: It is allowing yourself to be controlled by other people's thoughts.

Dr. Hora: That's right.

Comment: We consent to live in a dream.

Question: We consent to live in somebody else's dream?

Dr. Hora: That's right. And we believe that it is our dream. Most of the time we are hypnotized. Hypnotism is based on suggestibility. What is suggestibility? It is the belief of not having a mind of one's own.

Comment: There is also a belief that we have a mind of our own.

Dr. Hora: Then to have our own mind or not to have our own mind is the same. How could that be?

Comment: It is a belief in the power of personal minds, whether one's own or someone else's.

Dr. Hora: Suppose we have a so-called headstrong child who resists everything that she is being told and insists on having her way in everything. Is this child hypnotized or not? Since she seems to be resistant to being influenced, is she immune to hypnotism?

Comment: She is hypnotized by the idea that she has a personal mind of her own.

Dr. Hora: Right. Independent thinkers and so-called strong personalities are just as hypnotized as the so-called "weak-minded" people. There are some people who come across as very powerful or pig-headed. And there are independent thinkers who seem to be inaccessible to hypnotism; no one can tell them anything, and yet, they are also hypnotized.

Question: Where does this hypnotism come from?

Comment: Hypnotism indicates that we don't know who we really are, or what real mind is.

Question: But where does it come from?

Dr. Hora: It comes from "going up and down and to and fro" in the world. Like the flu, as the saying goes, there is a lot of it going around.

Comment: It is the so-called deceiver, the whisperer, the seducer, the adversary.

Dr. Hora: What then is the secret of becoming immune to hypnotism?

Comment: Knowing what we really are and who we are.

Dr. Hora: We have to come to understand that there is only one Mind—God—and this Mind controls everyone and everything that is real; and there is no other power or mind anywhere to exert an influence on us. Only God's thoughts constitute our being, and if we are aware of divine Mind's continuous influence on us we cannot be hypnotized. Garbage thoughts cannot lodge themselves in our consciousness, and we are safe. How can we attain such a realization? Is this an attractive idea? Is anyone drawn to this idea?

Comment: It is more that we are driven than drawn.

Dr. Hora: Yes, the idea of the one Mind is difficult to accept. We would all prefer to believe in having personal minds. Some people resist the idea of the one Mind so strongly that when the time comes for them to accept it, they go through a serious crisis, kicking up a fuss against having to die. They go into heaven kicking and screaming. The personal mind is enraged by the prospect of having to erase itself.

Question: What is personal mind made up of?

Dr. Hora: What is darkness made up of? Nothing.

Comment: Sometimes I think we die little by little, so what is that personal mind?

Dr. Hora: It is a belief which has to die. We have to come to realize that God is the only Mind, and that man cannot produce intelligent thoughts.

Comment: I get the impression that you are implying that I am some sort of a puppet at the end of a string, and all my thoughts and emotions are controlled by someone else.

Dr. Hora: Yes, we are puppets, but there are no strings.

Comment: At one time I thought this way, too. I saw myself as a dummy governed by the one Mind. That's a negative idea about God being in charge.

Dr. Hora: What do we mean when we say we are puppets without strings? Puppets on strings are designed to imply self-existence, apart from the puppeteer. But there is another form of puppetry where the puppet and the puppeteer are in full view, and the puppet serves only to express the thoughts and the qualities and the life of the puppeteer, so the puppet is an integral part of the puppeteer. The puppet and the puppeteer are one; there is no separation.

Comment: We have the choice to be puppets of God or puppets of hypnotism.

Dr. Hora: Yes. Being puppets of hypnotism can be very pathetic, like following trends in fashions, mannerisms, conforming to various silly fads. But when we are puppets of the divine Mind, then our true individuality, uniqueness, beauty, intelligence, and grace naturally become visible; then we are authentic and free. Self-realization is the realization of the reality of our true being.

Question: Is watching television a form of voluntary submission to hypnotism? I noticed that I have the habit of tuning in on certain programs regularly. Do you think this is harmful?

Dr. Hora: Only if you enjoy it.

Question: What does it mean if we enjoy it?

Dr. Hora: If we enjoy it, we get into the act and we are hypnotized. There is nothing wrong with watching television as long as we don't enjoy it. We can refuse to give our consent to being hypnotized, we are not helpless victims. When the Zen Master Suzuki said that the enlightened man walks two inches above the ground, he inferred that the enlightened man is not involved with the inanities of this world; he can observe them with a certain detachment. And if we can watch television that way, then we shall be safe from its hypnotic effects.

Question: What's the sense of watching television then?

Dr. Hora: Not much, except as a medium of information about the state of the world and the culture.

Dialogue No. 39

PROGRESS

Question: What is the value and meaning of man's constant quest for new horizons? My question is prompted by the recent successful landing of our instruments on the planet Mars.

Dr. Hora: Whenever we want to understand something, we approach it by asking two intelligent questions: "What is the meaning of what seems to be?" "What is what really *is?*"

Comment: The answer to the first question seems to me to be found in ambition; it would seem that man is infinitely ambitious.

Dr. Hora: Yes, there seems to be an insatiable ambition in man to explore ever wider horizons and overcome limitations. Now if we consider the second intelligent question, what answer can we expect? What really *is,* is God's infinite universe, the universe of Mind, and man engaged in an evolutionary process, seeking increasing understanding and eternally struggling to overcome his ignorance.

We are also making a great deal of progress on the spiritual plane and reaching to ever more distant horizons in terms of our understanding of spiritual reality. Our planetary travels are explorations of material reality. It is interesting to contemplate that material progress is the shadow of spiritual progress. And interestingly enough, spiritual progress is non-dual, whereas material progress is always dualistic, which means it is both good and evil. Being non-dual, spiritual progress is the infinite unfolding of God's good; material progress is the counterfeit appearance of this spiritual evolution. When Adam and Eve partook of the tree of knowledge, the serpent told them: "Ye shall be as gods, knowing good and evil" (Genesis 3:5). And, ever since then, there seems to be a parallel process going on; one is spiritual progress, the other is its shadow—the material counterfeit progress.

Question: Looking at the developments in the material world, can we find any value in it from a spiritual standpoint?

Dr. Hora: Inasmuch as it helps us to distinguish more clearly between shadow and substance, it is of value. Real progress is taking place in the individual and collective consciousness of mankind. The Bible describes how Jesus could transport himself from one place to another instantaneously. How are we to understand that? We could ask the question: "How long does it take to travel to the outer reaches of the universe in consciousness?"

Comment: It is instantaneous.

Dr. Hora: Yes. God is omnipresent life, love, and intelligence. What is omnipresent is simultaneously present everywhere. Therefore, it takes no time at all for us to travel to any part of the universe in consciousness. In the universe of Mind there is neither time nor space.

Comment: Last night I dreamed of a place overseas where I lived thirty years ago. I was clearly there; it couldn't have been more real if I had just arrived there by plane.

Dr. Hora: Jesus never built a rocketship, and yet he was light years ahead of the human race. We can be grateful for whatever material progress is being made, but we must understand that it always has within itself the seed of destruction. All material progress is both good and evil; therefore, it is not real, it is just shadow. Real progress is spiritual, and the entire human race is involved in it, whether consciously or unconsciously; the material phenomena which we call progress are just shadows of what is really going on.

Question: Are you saying that the shadow is of the same substance as the real?

Dr. Hora: What is the substance of a shadow? Nothing. Shadow is insubstantial; it is just an optical illusion. But the shadow is constantly keeping pace with the substance. It is very difficult for us to measure spiritual progress because PAGL is not quantifiable. PAGL is the measure of our spiritual progress.

Comment: We must also realize that the Bible says: "How

manifold are the works of the Lord"; that we are able to send instruments millions of miles away and make them responsive to our commands from the earth.

Dr. Hora: Certainly, a derivative form of creative intelligence is operating here, which is nothing to sneer at.

Question: Do you think it possible that a different type of spiritual being, in a different shape and form, may be found on Mars?

Dr. Hora: What is the shape and form of spiritual beings? They have no shape or form. What is the meaning of these agonizing questions? We are all agonizing over this question. We would like to have life appear in visible form; we are extremely desirous to touch life, to feel life, to see it, to weigh and measure it, to compare it, to cut it, to destroy it. But you see, life is consciousness; we are not the form we seem to be either—and that is hard to accept. Life is consciousness, and whatever is visible and tangible is just appearance.

Now we could ask: "What kind of appearances could we expect to find on Mars?" Only what we can imagine. We can never see anything that we cannot imagine, because everything that we see is only our imagination. What do the instruments on Mars see? We have received photographs from Mars, and what do these photographs show us? Mars is just what we expected it to be. What we cannot imagine, we cannot see; and what we cannot see, we cannot imagine. But whatever we imagine is purely imaginary. Now how will we ever get beyond this limitation? The Bible clearly says: "We look not at the things which are seen, but at the things which are not seen: for the things which are seen are temporal; but the things which are not seen are eternal" (II Corinthians 4:18).

Now how are we going to see something that is real? Besides imagination, there is *beholding.* What is the difference between imagining something and beholding something? You may have noticed that we never say: "Let us imagine God." God is unimaginable because God is infinite. And we cannot imagine the real man, either.

Comment: We would be using a faculty which is not real to apprehend reality.

Dr. Hora: Right. Beholding is the faculty which we all have —though it is not very widely known—with which we can discern the real. A photo camera cannot behold; it can only record light and shadow. Only man can behold. For instance, a portrait artist can paint a picture of an individual which a camera could never depict. How is that?

Comment: Because an artist can discern certain qualities which characterize the individual.

Dr. Hora: Right. The camera only portrays form, but the artist can see and portray qualities. The faculty of beholding enables us to discern that which has no form, and which is not accessible to sensory perception. Yet it constitutes the essential reality of individuals and all things in the universe. Therefore, if we want to know whether there is life on Mars, we must behold it. And we don't have to travel there, we can behold it from here. Since life is God, life is everywhere. Our work here essentially consists of awakening within ourselves the faculty of beholding so that we may see what is not seen and know what is real. And when we have succeeded in developing and awakening the faculty of beholding, then we are healed of all our problems and we are enlightened.

The Buddhists and Hindus speak of awakening the third eye, and we speak of the Christ-consciousness. Jesus could behold the spiritually perfect individual in a leper, a crippled man, a blind man, or even a dead man. And that beholding was so powerful that the shadow had to change to correspond to the substance. That was the essence of the miraculous healings which he performed.

So material progress moves in the direction of seeing more and more of what isn't, and spiritual progress is seeing more and more of what really is. There is a funny definition of a specialist as someone who learns more and more about less and less until he comes to know everything about nothing.

St. Paul said something which would sum up all that has been said until now: "The invisible things of him from the creation of the world are clearly seen, being understood by the things that are made, even his eternal power and Godhead" (Romans 1:20).

Dialogue No. 40

IS IT WORTH IT?

Comment: Yesterday I was attending a seder, which is a Jewish Passover celebration (the feast commemorating the exodus of the Jews from Egypt), and we were reading from a book known as a Haggadah. I came across something very interesting in it. There was a series of statements in it which went as follows: "The lazy child doesn't even take the trouble to ask a question; the stupid child is not interested; the foolish child asks, Why? But the wise child asks, What is the meaning?" It occurred to me that somebody else must have known this long before Dr. Hora. I was thrilled to find this.

Dr. Hora: And what does the "smart" child do?

Comment: He doesn't attend a seder!

Dr. Hora: The "smart" child asks questions which no one can answer.

Comment: Recently I was on a trip to a Caribbean island, and I was impressed by how beautifully nature is able to take care of itself without human intervention. I was wondering whether man is needed at all, and what might be the meaning and purpose of human existence.

Dr. Hora: This is one of those "smart" questions. Nevertheless, we may attempt to answer it later. Someone else asked a question that requires consideration. The question was: "Is it all worth it? Is it worthwhile to struggle for years to try to understand God?" This question reminds me of a man who was sitting in a cocktail lounge, feeling very depressed. He was only drinking coffee but he was sorely tempted to take a drink of liquor, except that he was on the spiritual path and knew better. As he looked around at other people who seemed to be having a good time imbibing alcohol, he asked himself: "Is this struggle worth it? Do I have to be on the spiritual path and be miserable, when only one drink would solve the whole problem?" But he didn't do it. Now the question can be asked again: "Is it really worth it?"

Comment: Of course it's worth it, because when the whiskey wears off—or, as in my case, the chocolate ice cream—you are back where you were before.

Dr. Hora: This is an interesting dilemma, one which life often puts before us. Are we going to live by short-term gain and long-term loss, or shall we forego the short-term gain in the hope of long-term salvation? And everyone has to make that choice either now or at some time in the future.

Comment: I used to be bothered by the question of whether there is meaning to life at all, but I have come to realize that my life is not meaningless because I have learned to understand the meaning of every problem I ever faced. I am very grateful for that.

Dr. Hora: Let us then correlate the first and the second question. The first question was: "Is there a purpose to human life?" The second question was: "Is it worth the trouble to find out?" What is the relationship between meaning and purpose? What is meaning and what is purpose?

Comment: Purpose seems to be an invalid idea; it smacks of cause-and-effect thinking.

Dr. Hora: Right. Purpose is a teleological cause, it is a "Why?" projected into the future. There is, however, a meaning to human existence, and there is a meaning to the human struggle which we are all going through—the struggle of attaining the realization of what is real. There is no way anyone could escape this journey, for sooner or later everyone has to come into conscious union with God. Life in the cocktail lounges, the massage parlors, the night clubs, as well as in hospitals, has one thing in common, namely, the celebration of the body as a source of pleasure and pain. This is a mockery of life and a state of blind ignorance. It is not possible to be preoccupied with thoughts of physical pleasure without sliding over into thoughts of physical pain, for these are two sides of the same coin. Spiritual growth and realization is the escape from the life which is anchored in the body, and leads to the discovery of the non-dual good. What is the non-dual good?

Comment: It has no opposite.

Dr. Hora: Right. In the history of man there were always people who were on the spiritual path and were sacrificing everything for it in the aspiration to achieve the non-dual good, the good which is real. These were called, among other things, seers, mystics, religious fanatics, ascetics, renunciates. Nowadays there are more people seeking the truth than ever before, and we happen to be among the blessed ones who have the opportunity to be on that path. Of course, to some people we may very well appear to be foolish.

Comment: Sometimes I wonder how anybody can get along without these principles we are learning.

Comment: Sometimes, when I observe self-indulgent people, I wonder whether they are suffering?

Dr. Hora: Perhaps you are just trying to comfort yourself with that idea.

Comment: I had parents who thought I would be healthier if I drank more. They thought I was missing out on all the fun because I didn't drink, they wanted me to be more "with it." But I never cared for it, and I thought that there was something wrong with me because I wasn't able to enjoy alcohol as much as my parents, who believed that being on the path was pathological, and that it was due to some sort of weakness in my character that I needed God.

Dr. Hora: There comes a point when it seems we cannot make further progress because we are reluctant to let go of some cherished indulgence. But at the same time, we cannot indulge ourselves because we are aware of the price to be paid. Sometimes we stagnate and struggle until such time that we make the radical step and decide to refuse to even think of it anymore—whatever it may be. Everyone has a private fantasy about what is good and desirable for him. It can be alcohol, sex, power, possessions, money, or fame. If we have the impression that we haven't made much progress lately, this may indicate an unwillingness to part with some secret cherished idea about what would give us happiness. Sometimes such stagnation results in a crisis which, in turn, forces us to give up our cherished idea; but it is preferable to give it up on the basis of wisdom rather than suffering.

Is It Worth It?

Every one of us has to wrestle with the angel, as Jacob did, and every one of us has to go through a "Red Sea experience," where one can neither go forward nor turn back. It is usually at this point that we hear the "murmurings of the children of Israel": "Was it worth it?"

Dialogue No. 41

COMPLETENESS

Dr. Hora: You seem to have a question.

Comment: Yes, but could you tell me what it is?

Dr. Hora: I think you want to know how to find a husband.

Comment: That's a good question.

Dr. Hora: In the kingdom of God they neither marry nor not marry. What is a marriage?

Comment: Funny that you should ask that. I ask myself this question every day. It seems to be a running battle, but not really. I am grateful to know that the battle is not with my husband but with my own thoughts.

Comment: I think a marriage between two individuals is a symbolic expression of their marriage to God, and there is really only one marriage, namely, conscious union with God. But I would really like to understand marriage between two individuals better.

Dr. Hora: Who invented marriage?

Comment: Man.

Question: What man?

Dr. Hora: Before Eve was taken out of the body of Adam, Adam must have had a woman inside of him, Adam must have been bisexual. When two people get married, what are they trying to do? They are trying to complete themselves. Does that mean that when we are not married we are half people, incomplete people, with no hope of ever becoming complete?

Comment: Looking at it from this standpoint, that would be the only logical conclusion.

Dr. Hora: So what is this tremendous drive in men and women to get together in a fusion reaction? We are trying to achieve completeness on a material level of existence, but this is very frustrating. In the light of this revelation, what would be the meaning of orgasm in the sexual act? It is the illusion of having attained completeness through fusion of the male and female principles. But illusions are always followed by disillusionments. So on the material level, things seem to be constantly separating themselves, trying to fuse, and not succeeding, all of which is very frustrating. Life is a constant state of short-lived illusory fulfillments. Furthermore, there are long periods of emptiness, longing, discontent, frustration and a sense of incompleteness. But we know that things are not the way they seem to be.

We have just described the meaning of what seems to be: the meaning of marriage; the meaning of the longing for fusion of the male and female; the meaning of the pleasure of orgasm, and of the unpleasant aftertaste of disillusionment. There is no such thing as a harmonious and satisfactory sex life. Anyone who would claim to have a good sex life is deceiving himself. There is no such thing because it is a dream, it is what seems to be. There is no such thing as a good marriage as long as two incomplete individuals are trying to fulfill themselves, to achieve completeness with the help of one another. On the material level man is condemned to eternal frustration whether he is married or unmarried. That is why in the kingdom of God they neither marry nor not marry.

Question: Does that mean that the human idea of marriage is not present in heaven?

Dr. Hora: That's right. What is present in the kingdom of God?

Comment: Individual completeness.

Dr. Hora: Right. Everyone is a complete individuality. What does the word "individuality" mean?

Comment: Undividedness.

Dr. Hora: That's right. In the kingdom of God we are individuals, we are complete, which means that the female has never been removed from the male, and the male has never been taken out of the female. God created man in his own image and likeness, male and female.

Question: What does male and female have to do with God?

Dr. Hora: God is male and female.

Comment: I don't see what the difference is between male and female in the eyes of God.

Dr. Hora: A man is capable of tenderness and love and

spiritual strength, and a woman is likewise capable of expressing such qualities. And maleness and femaleness are not
anatomical but spiritual. Both maleness and femaleness are
qualities of consciousness. Usually there is much resistance
to this idea because the desire for fusion is very strong in us.

Let us now consider whether the understanding of this
truth could enhance marital life? That's the question, isn't it?
If a theory is valid, it must have practical applications. Suppose a husband and a wife achieve an understanding that they
are two complete spiritual individualities. What will happen
to their marriage?

Comment: It will be harmonious.

Dr. Hora: Absolutely. There will be no more using one
another; there will be just joint participation in the good of
God. What will disappear is the great urge to use one another
for personal gratification, which leads to resentfulness and
many misunderstandings.

Question: Does affection have anything to do with love?

Dr. Hora: Affection is the human equivalent of love.

What we have said until now must not be construed as
implying what should be and what shouldn't be. We are
merely seeking to understand and clarify the meaning of what
seems to be in contrast to what really is. The more complete
an individual understands himself to be, the easier it will be
to live alongside of him. We could ask again: "What is the
meaning of maleness and femaleness?" Unless we understand
that, we will never come to terms with the human appearances. Whatever exists in the material world is an indication
of something that exists in spiritual reality. Since male and
female qualities apparently exist in the material world, we
have to account for it in spiritual reality. So we cannot say that
there is no male and female in divine reality. The material
world is a symbolic counterfeit representation of spiritual
reality.

Comment: The fact that we speak of God as Love-Intelligence may very well indicate the male and female principle
present in one.

Dr. Hora: What relevance does all this have to our need to understand the phenomena of the various sexual deviations so prevalent in our culture? There seem to be mannish women and effeminate men; there is homosexuality, lesbianism, bisexuality, and all sorts of combinations thereof. All phenomena are meaningful; therefore, we can understand them by discovering what they mean. Wouldn't it be a tremendous relief to someone who is agonizing over his sexual thoughts if he could be helped to understand that we are all male and female, and that there is nothing to be disturbed about if someone's sexual interests are prevalently male or female?

Suppose a man likes to wear female clothes, or a woman wants to get married to another woman. What does all this mean? Does it mean that they are criminals, or bad? Does it mean it shouldn't be that way? Does it mean that they had bad mothers? Does it mean that someone is to blame for it? Do we have to find out why they are that way, or what to do with them? These are individuals who are seeking completeness; they want to be complete individuals. And if this completeness is sought in a heterosexual relationship, it is socially acceptable and is considered normal. If a man is trying to complete himself by using a woman, that is approved by society; or if a woman is trying to complete herself by using a man, that is also all right. But if there are some deviations from this standard, the aim is still the same but the rules are not socially acceptable and it is condemned. If an individual comes to understand his spiritual completeness, then all his frantic search to complete himself on a material plane will cease, and he will be healed no matter what form his deviation may have taken. All that is needed is to realize our completeness as spiritual beings.

Comment: The simplicity of this understanding is overwhelming, especially if you consider the volumes of books that have been written on this subject. It is beautifully nonjudgmental and gentle, and anyone who hears this must be greatly relieved.

Dr. Hora: "Ye shall know the truth, and the truth shall make you free" (John 8:32).

Dialogue No. 42
SELF-ESTEEM

Question: Could we talk about self-esteem?

Dr. Hora: All right. What do we mean by self-esteem?

Comment: What is disturbing about the concept of self-esteem is the fact that it relates to the sense of selfhood; therefore, I would prefer to speak of a sense of self-assurance rather than self-esteem.

Dr. Hora: Self-esteem is a psychological concept, and assurance is the spiritual equivalent of it. Nevertheless, it is important to realize that self-esteem is very precious to all of us; of course, peace and assurance are even more precious. We could say that in order to have a sense of peace and assurance, we must first have self-esteem.

Comment: It is a certain regard one has for oneself. In working with children, it is particularly noticeable how important self-esteem is. There are children in my class who destroy their own work; they are unable to complete their assignments because they are convinced that whatever they do cannot possibly be good.

Dr. Hora: What is *chutzpah?*

Comment: It is nerve, arrogance, shameless audacity.

Comment: It is a false kind of self-esteem.

Dr. Hora: It is an erroneous way of endeavoring to establish self-esteem. Books could be written about the many ways in which people strive to establish self-esteem. And there are many ways in which people are often damaging their self-esteem, or having it damaged by their friends and enemies. Of course, a friend can damage it much more effectively than an enemy.

Question: Wouldn't self-esteem mean that you are taking credit for whatever good you do?

Dr. Hora: Not necessarily. Self-esteem is not synonymous with pride.

Comment: But we are often speaking about the importance of transcending the self.

Dr. Hora: Nevertheless, we must face the fact that the issue of self-esteem is a very important issue in everyone's life, even in those who claim to be spiritually enlightened. We must esteem the self correctly. When Jesus said "Love thy neighbor as thyself" he said, in effect, that you must esteem your neighbor correctly as you esteem yourself correctly. If we don't know how to esteem ourselves correctly, we don't know how to esteem others correctly. As a matter of fact, the lower the estimate of ourselves is, the more cruel, nasty, and hurtful we can be toward others. Many a rebel, criminal, sadist, or debasing personality is but an individual who has a damaged self-esteem, who is somehow trying to repair his own damaged sense of self by inflicting wounds on others. There is an infinite variety of problems which can flow from lack of self-esteem, or diminished or damaged self-esteem. Sexual problems, anxiety reactions, chronic hostility, vindictiveness, chronic depression, can all be connected with the issue of inadequate self-esteem.

Question: What is the relationship between self-confirmatory ideation and the issue of self-esteem?

Dr. Hora: Well, let us take as an example a lady who gets a mink coat; does that contribute to her self-esteem?

Comment: Yes.

Dr. Hora: No. It is just a self-confirmatory act, an endeavor to bolster the sense of self-esteem through artificial means. Another form of seeking to repair damaged self-esteem is ambition. Many a successful individual was driven to achieve success by a desire to improve his self-esteem. There is a well-known novel called *What Makes Sammy Run?* It depicts a Hollywood character whose ambition was enormous and who drove himself to success and ultimately to failure. The damaged self-esteem is never really repaired.

Comment: The harder you try, the worse it gets.

Dr. Hora: These are just misdirected efforts at repair. Fame has been achieved, fortunes have been made, but peace and assurance and love have not been found. This reminds us of a story of a man who came to a psychiatrist and said: "If I had two million dollars, I wouldn't need you." When the psychiatrist asked him why exactly two million, he said: "Because one million I got, but it don't do me no good!" He was talking about money, but the real issue was self-esteem.

Self-esteem is a psychological problem that we all face. It has only a spiritual solution; if we don't understand this, we can spend many, many years—perhaps all of our lives—trying to heal this psychological problem through psychological means. But this is not possible, for it can only be healed spiritually.

Comment: I don't think we have answered the question raised, namely: "What is the difference between self-confirmatory ideation and self-esteem."

Question: Is it paying attention to the wrong self?

Dr. Hora: The difference is subtle. In self-confirmatory ideation we may pursue a self-deprecatory direction—for instance, if we invite someone to hurt us or debase us. It diminishes our self-esteem while it confirms our sense of self.

Comment: In other words, something negative or unwholesome can also be self-confirmatory.

Dr. Hora: Self-confirmatory thinking is not synonymous with the striving to improve one's self-esteem. The solution is, of course, spiritual. You may already suspect that all problems are psychological; but all solutions are spiritual.

Question: When you say that all problems are psychological, do you mean that they are just fantasy?

Dr. Hora: Yes, you could say that.

Comment: They all stem from thoughts.

Dr. Hora: They are thoughts. The concept of the right man exemplifies the solution to the problem of self-esteem and to the problem of self-confirmatory ideation. *The right man is a spiritual presence manifesting wisdom and love derived from God, the all-knowing Mind.* When we discover who we are and what we are, then all these problems disappear, and self-esteem becomes a right appreciation of the truth of being. What is the practical import of what we were saying until now? What practical consequences will it have for us after we leave here tonight?

Comment: Our lives will be more harmonious, and we will be more effective in the world.

Dr. Hora: We will be healed of fear and of courage. Would you believe that? Is it good to be healed of courage?

Comment: Courage is the same as fear; if there were no fear, there would be no need for courage.

Dr. Hora: Right. But the world values courage greatly.

Comment: Because it is a psychological solution to fear.

Dr. Hora: Does a courageous man think of God when he is being courageous?

Comment: He is thinking about how brave he is.

Dr. Hora: The point we are trying to make is that there is something better than courage. As with self-esteem, courage is a psychological solution to a psychological problem. Self-esteem and courage could also be considered psychological virtues, but we must not be satisfied with them for there is something better. Pride and courage must be replaced by peace, assurance, gratitude, and love.

There is a movement called Ethical Culture. It aspires to morality, ethics, and all the psychological virtues. But without a spiritual basis, these things are like houses built on sand; they cannot sustain the stresses of life. It is very difficult to be an ethical, moral, and virtuous individual without God.

Dialogue No. 43

INTERACTION OR OMNIACTION?

Comment: I seem to need something to turn me around because lately I am very apathetic.

Dr. Hora: What is apathy?

Comment: Disinterest.

Dr. Hora: When we feel defeated, we feel passionless; we have to then pull ourselves together. It is like getting up in the morning when we would rather stay in bed and dream a little longer. We have to rouse ourselves. The Bible says: "Gird up thy loins" (II Kings 4:29, 9:1; Job 38:3; 40:7; Jeremiah 1:17). We have to turn to God in prayer and refuse to be seduced into mental apathy, which is a passive state of misery. Jesus said: "What I say unto you I say unto all, Watch" (Mark 13:37). Let us not sink into the swamp of apathy and self-pity. Straighten up, don't slouch, and be assured that God is present. Remind yourself who you really are. You are not a person among other persons, having to cope with the world alone, or cope with problems all by yourself.

One of the great mysteries of human experience is the idea of interaction. We see life as interaction between ourselves and other people. This impression is so convincing that it is universally assumed to be a fact. We see interactions between mother and child, husband and wife, employer and employee, friend and foe; everything seems to be based on interaction. But in reality there is no such thing as interaction. Would you believe that?

Comment: That's hard to believe.

Dr. Hora: There is only omniaction.

Comment: We saw a lot of interaction on television when we watched the proceedings of the political conventions.

Dr. Hora: What do we mean by omniaction? In apathy there is inaction. Inaction seems to be a form of interaction; unsatis-

factory interaction can throw us into inaction. In reality, however, there is neither inaction nor interaction, there is only
omniaction. How can we make such a claim? Isn't it absurd?

Interaction is based on the impression that there are many
minds and many powers in the world. But when we come to
understand the great truth that there is only one Mind, one
Power in the whole universe, and that this Mind is omnipresent, omnipotent, omniscient, and omniactive, manifesting itself in an infinite number of ways, then we will see the fact that
there is only omniaction—the divine Mind expressing itself
through an infinite variety of individualities which are always
intelligent, loving, and good. We suddenly discover a new
freedom. We realize we do not depend on anyone, just as we
do not make anyone depend on us. Everything is already
taken care of. Our good does not come *from* people, though
it may come *through* people. Understanding this gives us a
great sense of assurance and freedom.

The basic premise of psychiatry is that it entails the man-
agement of the interaction between doctor and patient. But,
actually, there is no such thing. Those of you who have caught
glimpses of this truth know that there is really no interaction
between doctor and patient; there is only the activity of the
truth in consciousness.

Comment: The truth is being allowed in.

Dr. Hora: Exactly. And the same truth which governs the
psychiatrist also governs the patient. Doctor and patient
jointly participate in the truth of omniactive Mind; and that
truth has the power to solve every problem, heal every disease, bring harmony, joy, vigor, and vitality to the apathetic.

Question: Suppose a mother has trouble interacting with her
child, how could this help the situation?

Dr. Hora: If there is no interaction and there is only omniaction, what happens?

Comment: There is no conflict.

Dr. Hora: Both mother and child have a chance to become
what they really are, namely, perfect reflections of a perfect
God. It is the illusion of interaction which creates the appearance of distortions in life with which we are constantly con-

fronted. For instance, lately it has become fashionable for people to go to sex therapy clinics where they are being taught how to interact successfully with their sex partners in the sexual act. This has developed into a complex science. Sex is looked upon as an eminent form of interaction between a man and a woman. As a result of that, it has become a very complicated process involving many technical considerations. Sex has become so complicated that volumes of books are being written about how it should and should not be practiced. The basic assumption is that sex is interaction. But, contrary to general opinion, real sex is an event; it is not one person doing something to another, it is just the omniactive Mind expressing itself as love. It is a harmonious event, taking place simultaneously between two people who are in harmony with life and love, and who jointly participate in it. That is real sex; everything else is not sex but a misinterpretation based on the impression that life is a process of interaction.

As we realize the truth of omniaction in contrast to interaction, we shall find life becoming increasingly simple and harmonious, because only if there is no interaction can we become what we really are.

Comment: Presence instead of person.

Dr. Hora: Right. Instead of personalities, we become spiritual presences. The Zen Master says: "In the realm of the real, there is neither self nor other, there is only that which really *is.*" If there is neither self nor other, then there is no interaction possible, there is only the continuous manifestation of Love-Intelligence as vigor, vitality, goodness, joy, perfection.

Question: Are you just perceiving the good continuously unfolding and you being part of it?

Dr. Hora: Yes. Our thought processes undergo a radical change. We are completely liberated from thoughts of what should be or shouldn't be, and we are aware of the good which already is. At this point it is helpful to realize that we have not said that interaction shouldn't be and omniaction should be. What was said is that interaction is not and omniaction is. Interaction seems to be, but is not; omniaction doesn't seem to be, but is. Blessed is the man who can see that omniaction really *is.*

Comment: I can see omniaction in nature quite easily.

Dr. Hora: Right. We don't have to make a tree grow, it grows. Material life is a dream, the dreamer is also a dream. Our dream is that we are living in interaction with other people. But there is only the omnipresence of omniactive, omniscient Mind manifesting itself in an infinite variety of ways, always intelligent, always loving, always good, and always harmonious. Even to catch a little glimpse of this truth will instantaneously heal every problem.

Comment: I don't understand the word "active" in omniactive. Could you explain it, please?

Dr. Hora: The word "active" indicates the dynamism of Mind which is expressing itself as a governing principle in the universe. Let us take, for instance, a tree. If we observe a tree in the spring when the sap is beginning to flow, we can see the activity of this vital force pushing for manifestation with great power.

Comment: Like a blade of grass breaking through a crack in the pavement.

Dr. Hora: Right. So there is dynamism to life, to divine Mind, and this dynamism is an activity expressing itself in myriads of individual life forms which bear witness to this force. In every blade of grass, every flower, every tree, the same force is actively expressing itself.

Comment: But a tree doesn't have an ego.

Dr. Hora: Man has no ego either; God, Mind is his ego. Once we realize that there is no interaction, then it becomes clear that infinite Mind is the ego of everyone; God is the "I AM" of all of us, just as God is the same vital force pressing for manifestation in every flower, plant, or other life form everywhere in the universe.

Question: What about habit? Is man a creature of habit? What is the remedy to habit?

Dr. Hora: "If any man be in Christ, he is a new creature: old things are passed away; behold, all things are become new"

(II Corinthians 5:17). There is no reality to habits, because omniaction is forever new.

Question: In the place where I work I am exposed to a great deal of intimidation; how could I be freed from this unpleasantness?

Dr. Hora: Intimidation is a form of interaction. What would life be like without interaction?

Comment: It would feel like nonexistence.

Comment: Better intimidation than nothing at all.

Comment: If you see yourself as a human person rather than a child of God, then you need interaction in order to confirm yourself. But if you know who you truly are, then you don't need interaction and life would not be boring.

Dr. Hora: What is there if there is no interaction?

Comment: There is the harmony and joy of omniaction.

Dr. Hora: Right. Could you explain what omniaction is?

Comment: God flowing freely through us.

Dr. Hora: Is this possible? Is life without interaction possible? What is interaction, really? Interaction is really a dream.

Comment: It is based on a belief of many powers.

Dr. Hora: I was reminded today of a passage from the Bible which says: "The leaves of the tree were for the healing of the nations" (Revelation 22:2). What could this mean? We shall suddenly understand it if we ask one question: Is there interaction among the leaves of a tree?

Comment: No.

Dr. Hora: Right. Absolutely not. The leaves of a tree have no interrelationships with one another. What is there among the leaves of a tree? There is joint participation in the life of the tree, and every individual leaf expresses the qualities of that life which is the tree. What is the meaning of the claim that the leaves of the tree are for the healing of nations? If nations would understand life as omniaction, there would be healing of strife, discord, and even wars. There would be only the glorious, harmonious omniaction of that life force of which we are individualized expressions. So the secret of harmonious life as individuals, groups, families, and nations is the realization that there is no such thing as interaction, for that is a dream. It doesn't really exist. If there is no such thing

as interaction, then there can be no seduction, no* provocation, no intimidation.

Now the question may be asked: "What practical value is
there in exploring this truth?" Can we stop other people from
interacting with us? Yes and no. Let us remember that nothing comes into experience uninvited. If there is no thought of
interaction in our consciousness, there will be no interaction
experiences. All that is needed is to erase all thoughts of
interaction and replace them with the grateful acknowledg-
ment that all there is, is the activity of divine Love in consciousness. The leaves of the tree are for the healing of all
conflicts. So if we can see ourselves to some extent as individual leaves on a tree, then we are jointly participating in the
love of God. We will live harmoniously alongside one another, never trespassing upon one another. Have you ever
seen a sun ray colliding with another sun ray, interacting with
another sun ray? Somehow man has fallen asleep and has
begun to dream about interaction; that happened a long time
ago, and we are still dreaming this dream. "Awake thou that
sleepest, and arise from the dead, and Christ shall give thee
light" (Ephesians 5:14).

Comment: But interaction is exciting, and life without interaction would seem dull and boring. Nobody would notice
you, you would be just like another leaf on a tree.

Dr. Hora: An Indian guru once said: "I am studying to be
nobody." Most people don't like this idea. Certainly, unenlightened man is terribly concerned with being somebody—
with being noticed, with being acknowledged, with being admired, with being recognized, with being loved. Everyone
seems to have this desire from early childhood on all the way
till late childhood, even very late childhood. Now the question
is: "If we give up this wonderful thing, what will there be
left?" Is there any compensation for it? What is the reward of
being enlightened?

Comment: PAGL.

Dr. Hora: Is PAGL enough? Can it compete with gold med-
als and stars? And persecutions? What is the compensation
that would make it worthwhile for us?

Comment: Freedom, fearlessness.

Dr. Hora: Right. Freedom and fearlessness. Some of you may have seen the Grand Canyon or some other magnificent natural beauty. When we see something extremely beautiful and grand, we are not thinking about getting recognition or being admired (unless we are very sick), but we lose awareness of ourselves in this great sight. It is a supremely uplifting occasion to see, for instance, a beautiful sunset. The reward for losing the pleasures and pains of interaction is the ability to see God in action. What do we see when we see God in action?

Question: The beauty of the sunset. Is it nature or is it God?

Dr. Hora: The sunset is nature, the beauty is God. When we see God, we see beauty, harmony, goodness, love, purity, wisdom, perfection, joy—everything that is really worthwhile. When we wake up from the dream of interaction, we begin to see God.

Dialogue No. 44

INNOCENCE

Comment: I wish I were more interested in financial gain. I heard about law school graduates who, when they come out of Harvard Law School, get jobs with salaries beginning at $25,000 a year. I could do the same work they do but I don't earn that much money. Somehow, I am thinking of putting God and spiritual interests aside and go for the money.

Dr. Hora: What's your question?

Comment: She wants to know how to be happy without the spiritual.

Dr. Hora: Is that the question?

Comment: The nagging question is, how can I get rid of this beckoning which money has for me?

Comment: Dr. Hora will now tell us how to get rich.

Comment: There are people who are happy who don't have much money and who don't live in the style I want to live in.

Dr. Hora: What style do you want to live in?

Comment: Someone to cook meals for me and drive me around when I want to be driven around.

Comment: Then you need more than a million dollars.

Dr. Hora: No, all you need is to become a wheelchair case.

Comment: That's not so funny!

Dr. Hora: This shows you how dangerous it is to fantasize. As Emerson said: "Beware of what you set your heart on, for you may get it."

Comment: This is interesting in view of the fact that you were recently on a cruise, chaperoning a young woman who was in a wheelchair.

Dr. Hora: The Bible says: "The love of money is the root of all evil" (I Timothy 6:10). Does that mean it is wrong to desire to be happy? No.

Comment: In our Declaration of Independence we are given the right to pursue happiness.

Dr. Hora: Right. But we don't say: "Enjoy the pursuit of happiness." We say: "Enjoy happiness." Happiness does not have to be pursued, happiness is to be realized. Happiness already is; we already are infinitely affluent and infinitely happy. It is important to realize that people who pursue happiness will never be happy; they will just be busy pursuing it and it will forever elude them. And yet, it is the will of God for all of us to be happy all the time.

Question: Aren't these fantasies caused by frustration?

Dr. Hora: Many people—those who ask "Why?"—reason that way. If they find themselves fantasizing, they ask: "Why am I fantasizing?" And the answer they give themselves is: "Because I am frustrated." And then they ask: "Why am I frustrated?" The answer is: "Because I cannot get what I want."

Let us consider the question: "What is better, to be affluent or to have a lot of money?"

Comment: To be affluent.

Dr. Hora: Can you explain?

Comment: Affluence is spiritual, it is knowing where your supply is coming from.

Dr. Hora: Right. Affluence is the consciousness of the unlimited flow of God's good. When we are conscious of that flow, we are wealthy, healthy, and wise.

Comment: If we are affluent, then money is no object; but if we are rich, money is always the object.

Dr. Hora: If we are affluent, we have everything we need in abundance. Money cannot buy affluence, but affluence can manifest itself even financially. What does a law degree have to do with affluence? Can a degree from Harvard Law School make us affluent? Do you need a college education for affluence? Certainly not. What do we need to be affluent? We need to understand where the good comes from and how it comes. What role does fantasy play in attaining affluence?

Comment: It is a barrier.

Dr. Hora: Right. Fantasy is the monkey wrench which makes it impossible to become affluent. Everyone has the tendency

to fantasize, even enlightened people, except that our enlightenment gives us the power to refuse to fantasize. Who are we
refusing when we refuse to fantasize?

Comment: The Devil.

Dr. Hora: When we are inclined to fantasize, we cannot
blame it on a cause; fantasizing doesn't have a cause, it is just
a sign that we are being tempted. And what can we do then?
We can say to the devil: "Go to hell, that's where you came
from and that's where you belong." And we overcome the
temptation.

Comment: I now realize that I really don't need anything
besides the good of God. I suddenly see that the good of God
really *is.*

Dr. Hora: We have just witnessed a successful case of "exor-
cism." Praise the Lord!

Comment: All this reminds me of the seventy-third Psalm,
where this whole issue is beautifully described in the most
inspiring poetry.

Dr. Hora: So let us not pursue happiness anymore, even if
it is in the Constitution. I am sure that the founding fathers
would see it our way if we had a chance to explain what we
mean, namely, that happiness cannot be pursued but, rather,
has to be realized.

Comment: That's what they meant, anyway.

Dr. Hora: Yes. What are we conscious of when we are
happy?

Comment: God's goodness.

Dr. Hora: Peace, assurance, gratitude, and love. Now the
question is: "How do we realize the happiness and affluence
that already is?" As long as we pursue happiness, we are in
a "should" mode of thinking; we say to ourselves, happiness
should be. "Should" thinking is a semantic trap. How does
the realization of happiness and affluence come about? What
is required for such realization to obtain in consciousness?
We have to cultivate an appreciation of spiritual good, and we
have to understand it. And then we shall be able to fulfill the
first commandment, which is crucial for happiness: "Thou
shalt have no other interest before the good of God." In order

to realize something successfully there must be an abiding interest in it.

As we are seeking to realize the good of God, we become more and more innocent intellectually, not naïve but innocent. What is the difference between naïveté and innocence? In the lion's den Daniel told the king: God has found innocency in me, and I was saved. ("Forasmuch as before him [God] innocency was found in me . . ." Daniel 6:22). Innocence can be defined as the absence of the arrogance of learning, which makes us receptive to spiritual truths. There are educated people who are deeply offended by the mention of the word "God." Now what is naïveté? A naïve individual is not innocent, he is just insufficiently sophisticated in the ways of the world.

Innocence is highly desirable. Essentially, it is intellectual humility. Einstein was a highly educated man but he was free of the arrogance of learning. There is a story about Einstein: he used to meet a little schoolgirl in front of his house. He became acquainted with her and she told him she had difficulties with mathematics. Whereupon Einstein said to her: "I will teach you mathematics if you pay me for it." The little girl asked how much she would have to pay, and Einstein said: "Well, you will have to give me your jelly beans for every lesson."

Comment: He was so humble he wou dn't presume to offer to teach her for nothing, which would have been a condescension.

Dr. Hora: Right.

Comment: Innocence has a purity about it which is most appealing.

Dr. Hora: Furthermore, innocence confers on us invulnerability. Daniel represents an example of the invulnerability of a consciousness which is innocent. The wild beasts represent the beastly mentalities of the people around him which had no power to hurt him.

Comment: This reminds me of the other story about Einstein in which he is supposed to have said: "Arrows of hate have been shot at me many times, but somehow they never hurt me because they came from a world with which I had nothing in common."

Dr. Hora: Ordinarily, we confuse innocence with naïveté. Naïveté is supremely vulnerable; it is dangerous to be naïve. But innocence is invulnerable. How about knowledgeableness? Knowledgeableness is not only vulnerable but it actually invites attack. Knowledgeableness and the arrogance of learning attract harm. Naiveté is susceptible to hurt and innocence is invulnerable. In Taoistic literature we read that the enlightened man has no place in himself where a poisoned arrow could get lodged.

So now we know how to be happy, how to be affluent, and how to be invulnerable.

Comment: Who could ask for anything more?

YES IS GOOD—NO IS ALSO GOOD

Question: What does it mean when one is unable to forgive? I want to forgive and I keep talking to myself about forgiveness, but I don't seem to be able to.

Comment: The inability to forgive seems to be connected with blaming. But if we are willing to shift the blame onto ignorance, then the personal feelings disappear.

Comment: I tried to do it that way, but it still doesn't work.

Dr. Hora: Sometimes we say that we cannot forgive someone, but actually the issue is not really forgiveness, the issue is wanting something.

Comment: Wanting what we believe should be.

Dr. Hora: That's right. Suppose we think that someone should love us and we feel that they don't, or that they love us the wrong way or not enough. Then we may mistake this problem for the issue of forgiveness. Actually, the issue is not forgiveness but a desire. We usually cannot have what we want, but if we managed to get what we want, it would turn into disaster. At best we can have what we would like. So it is possible that in this case the issue is not how to forgive someone, but how to get what we want.

Comment: And if we cannot get what we want, we blame.

Dr. Hora: How can we be healed of wanting?

Comment: Perhaps we must understand what we need.

Dr. Hora: In this case we need to let go of wanting. How can we not want what we want? Suppose we want a new car and we cannot get it. What is the difference between "I want" and "I would like"?

Comment: No difference at all.

Comment: I think there is a great difference. When we say, "I want" it is demanding, arrogant; whereas "I would like" allows it to happen or not to happen.

Dr. Hora: That's right. When we say "I want," there is no place for God in it; therefore, we can never really have what we want. But if we say, "I would like"—and if we say it with understanding—then what are we really saying? We are saying: "They will be done." What does that mean? Is it a religious cliché? Yes, but if we can penetrate into its real meaning, it becomes something very beautiful.

Comment: It means God knows best.

Dr. Hora: If we understand God as Infinite Love, the Principle of Supreme Intelligence, then we can calmly say, "If yes, good; if no, also good." Is this going to make us lackadaisical, more or less apathetic, or will it make us fatalistic? ("What will be, will be.") What is the difference between fatalism and accepting the will of God? If we accept the will of God, we are sure that only good can come into our lives—even though we may not be the ones to define what is good. But if we are fatalistic or lackadaisical, then we have accepted the notion that evil can also come into our lives and we have no choice, we are just sitting ducks in the devils's shooting gallery, and we can get either lucky or be afflicted with some form of evil. What a desperate outlook on life that is! If God says "No" to something we would like, we can be sure that it is in our interest; and if God says "Yes" to something we would like, we can be sure that it is a blessing.

Question: How does one improve one's ability to discern the will of God?

Dr. Hora: First of all, we must never say "I want." If we say "I want a car," we will not get it; and if we should get it, it will turn out to be a lemon. A teen-ager insisted on getting a red Camaro and, after much fighting with his parents, he finally got one. Two weeks later the entire transmission, among other things, went wrong and there was no end to aggravations. We must realize that we are not just playing on words here; it is serious, and it is important to learn to think right about our desires and needs. To want something is arrogant and willful, and this kind of ignorance invites trouble.

So we prefer to say "I would like," or "There seems to be a need for a means of transportation, and since it is my Father's good pleasure to supply every legitimate need, I can expect to find one that will meet my need." This way we bring ourselves into alignment with infinite Love-Intelligence which makes it possible for the whole process to be a harmonious unfolding of events.

Dialogue No. 46

ON BEING HELPFUL

Question: What is the wisdom of allowing people to live in ignorance? As you know I am a social worker and one of my clients is a woman whom I visit from time to time. I thought I was offering her good insight into what was troubling her, what the problem was between her and her son, but I think she is a little upset with me for trying to get this point across. It seems to me that I am trying to help, but I don't think she appreciates it. This reminded me that I heard you say: "It is all right to let people live in ignorance." But I never understood the wisdom behind that.

Dr. Hora: Is it all right to let people live in ignorance?

Comment: This question implies that we have control over other people.

Dr. Hora: Right. So then is it not all right?

Comment: It is not our decision to make.

Comment: You always said that only if we are asked to help can we offer help.

Dr. Hora: Yes. What then is the correct attitude toward ignorance?

Comment: I think I heard you say that it is all right to be wrong.

Dr. Hora: No, it is not all right to be wrong.

Comment: I think you said that people have a right to be wrong.

Dr. Hora: We don't say that it is all right to let people live in ignorance; we say that we respect people's right to live in ignorance if they want to, because unsolicited solicitude is tyranny. Were you being tyrannical, by any chance, toward your client?

Comment: I thought I was being helpful.

Comment: Our younger son was waiting all summer for a job

stringing tennis rackets in a sporting goods store. Finally, last week he was called to work, and he strung six rackets the first day. After he came home from work, he got a telephone call from the manager of the store who said to him: "You fouled up all six rackets and you are fired." This was a very big shock to our son, and I was in a dilemma about whether I had the right to try to help him, since he didn't ask me.

Comment: Sometimes even if someone asks for help, he may not really mean it.

Dr. Hora: Yes, we have to make sure whether the individual really means it. The Chinese sage Lao-tse said: "The truthful man I believe, but the liar I also believe, and thereby the truth is revealed." What does that mean? He describes a way of dealing with people. If someone is lying to us, we have no business telling him that he is lying because that would be unsolicited solicitude.

Question: Suppose we just don't believe him?

Dr. Hora: If we don't believe him, we are implying that he is a liar, and that amounts to trying to be helpful in an unsolicited way. We must be very careful not to help unless sincerely asked. We have no right to reform people against their will, even if we are social workers.

Question: Suppose people say to us: "I am smart, I am stupid, I am powerful, I am sick," and so on?

Dr. Hora: These are self-confirmatory statements and we have to respect people's right to engage in self-confirmatory ideation.

Question: What is the meaning of being annoyed with such people?

Dr. Hora: That means that we are meddlers or busybodies. What is a busybody?

Comment: Someone who mind's everybody's business.

Dr. Hora: Or we may be amateur psychologists. It is, however, our business to see through all these things and be aware and alert. Jesus said: "Go ye into all the world, and preach the gospel to every creature" (Mark 16:15). "Heal the sick, cleanse the lepers, raise the dead, cast out devils" (Matthew 10:8). How do we reconcile this with what we just said?

Comment: It has been mentioned here before that a beneficial presence in the world is helpful to others.

Dr. Hora: It would seem that here we have explicit instructions to go into the world and do certain specific things.

Comment: I don't think Jesus meant for the disciples to go out into the world and advertise their beliefs or foist them on others.

Dr. Hora: Many well-meaning Christian missionaries and evangelists got themselves into trouble by taking this literally, and lacking the understanding of its existential meaning, they tried to offer unsolicited solicitude.

Question: But if Jesus didn't mean it literally, then what did he mean? What was the real directive?

Dr. Hora: In the light of our present-day understanding, it simply means to be a beneficial presence in the world. And a beneficial presence is a shining light which attracts people's interest and can illuminate—upon request—the meaning of all problems and their solutions.

Comment: You sometimes say that we must be models of spiritual excellence, and you also said at one time that when Jesus was healing someone, he was just there and his understanding of the individual's true identity as a spiritual child of God was so clear that he didn't have to say a word. The purity of his consciousness healed the people and dissolved their problems.

Dr. Hora: Right. It is then not an operational process but an existential one. The above biblical quotations must be understood in the context of their existential implication.

According to Taoist formulation, a beneficial presence in the world is engaged in "action which is nonaction." According to our present-day formulations, we have been talking about *omniaction in contrast to interaction.* Operationalism is, of course, eminently based on the idea of interaction.

Question: By interaction you mean interpersonal action?

Dr. Hora: Yes. When we have an operational approach to life—which most of us are inclined to have—we are endeavoring to do something to someone else, to change his ignorance into understanding, for instance. This is interaction. We also call it "horizontal thinking." But, of course, Jesus was much too enlightened to see life in terms of interaction. Not many theologians realize this, but Jesus certainly must have seen life in terms of the omniaction of omnipotent, omniscient, and omnipresent divine Mind, the harmonizing principle of the universe. So he didn't have to do anything, he allowed God to act through him and around him and in him and everywhere in the universe. Thereby ignorance was and is being constantly healed and abolished.

Comment: This reminds me of a book I saw recently which tells "how to make a church grow through effective interpersonal ministry."

Dr. Hora: A lot of suffering may come from the well-meaning desire to improve other people. How does this apply to teaching, for instance, in schools?

Comment: Most teachers consider interpersonal relationships the basis of so-called "good teaching." In some schools teachers are rated on the quality of their interaction with their students.

Comment: Not many people would respect the child's right not to learn.

Comment: Of course no school and no parent would ever accept that idea.

Comment: But as long as we believe that a child does not have the right to not learn, we cannot be good teachers.

Comment: You wouldn't want to tell this to the children, of course.

Dr. Hora: What would it indicate if you wanted to tell this to the children? It would indicate that you don't believe it. It is like telling your child "I love you"; it means that you don't.

Comment: If we really love, it manifests itself.

Dr. Hora: Right. It is interesting that if we know about something and don't like it or just believe it, we like to talk about it.

Question: Is that what is called proselytizing?

Dr. Hora: Yes, of course. A good teacher would understand all this, and it would be implicit in his attitude in the classroom. As a result, there would be a climate of freedom and love in which children could really learn. Paradoxically enough, if a student's right not to learn is respected, he will learn.

Comment: This is the only place where talking and sharing insights is helpful.

Dr. Hora: Yes, because most of you are here more or less voluntarily. If you find this surprising, I will tell you a secret. Nobody goes to a psychiatrist entirely voluntarily. At first, one is driven by suffering; later on we are drawn by a desire for learning.

Comment: One thing puzzles me; suppose someone comes here and for months or even years doesn't really want help. It seems to me that Dr. Hora would not be upset by this. But if I, as a social worker or counselor, were in a situation where an individual sat in my presence and I perceived that he or she did not want any help, I think it would bother me very much. I would be inclined to try to persuade this individual and pressure him. What could be the meaning of this?

Dr. Hora: All right, let us explore this issue. What could be the meaning of the fact that someone would get upset if his solicitude is not being appreciated?

Comment: In one case the therapist allows the patient to be, and in the other case he doesn't allow him to be. It is a question of relationships again.

Dr. Hora: Such a situation is usually painful if one is in a helping profession and one's help is not appreciated. But it is even more painful to be a parent and to know what the child needs and what is true. One wants desperately to help the child, to protect him from hurting himself, and the child is unreceptive to this parental solicitude. This can really be very upsetting.

Comment: But I don't think that a therapist just sits there and doesn't care.

Dr. Hora: Right. But we are talking now about a situation where the helper is suffering more than the "helpee." What is the meaning of that?

Comment: The helper is personally involved.

Comment: The helper needs help.

Dr. Hora: Indubitably.

Comment: The helper and the helpee are one.

Dr. Hora: Yes, they have the same problem. If the helper is upset over the resistance of the helpee, they participate in the same problem. And what is the problem? The problem is vanity.

Comment: What makes you say that?

Dr. Hora: If we understand that vanity is a desire for admiration, then we realize that the helper wants to be admired for helping. The helpee, who is also vain, says: "I don't need you because I am just as smart as you are."

Comment: I just don't understand this. After all, the patient is seeking help! He is coming to see the helper.

Dr. Hora: Not really. As a matter of fact, in the case we started with today, the patient wasn't even coming to see the social worker; the social worker was going to see the client.

Comment: Yes, I have been visiting this woman once a month for about a year, and recently she said to me: "You may not know this, but I think I am helping you."

Dr. Hora: We see here a situation where interaction is taking place on the plane of vanity. And what happens there? Nothing, absolutely nothing. There is a stalemate; the helper wants to establish his own superiority, and the helpee refuses to be a helpee for the same reason.

Question: So what is the solution?

Dr. Hora: This stalemate is almost like a marriage where there is a "locking of horns" in interaction. The solution is in redefining the situation in terms of joint participation in the good of God. In this situation man is not a helper, he is a helpful being. What is the difference?

Comment: To help suggests some kind of activity, but to be helpful implies being filled with the potential of helping when asked.

Dr. Hora: To help is operational, to be helpful is existential.

Question: Does it mean being in whatever way seems helpful? Is the emphasis on being rather than on doing?

Dr. Hora: Yes. Is that clear?

Question: What did Jesus mean by saying "cleanse the lepers"?

Dr. Hora: What does leprosy stand for?

Comment: Wasn't it the most fearful and.most contagious disease?

Dr. Hora: At that time it stood for the epitome of impurity. Today we don't use that symbol anymore, today we have other symbols of impurity. Symbols keep changing with time and perspective. Jesus said: "The Father that dwelleth in me, he doeth the works" (John 14:10). Do you realize that?

Comment: Yes, but I don't like it.

Comment: I heard that a neurotic is someone who says, "I know that two and two is four, but I don't like it."

Dr. Hora: What's the fun in being a social worker if God gets all the credit?

Question: Would you say that, in order to be a beneficial social worker, one has to unlearn one's social work education?

Dr. Hora: No, the word here is "transcend." We don't have to unlearn anything but we can transcend it, which means we can go beyond what we have learned in school and beyond conventional thinking.

Dialogue No. 47

PARAMETERS OF PROGRESS

Question: Dr Hora, could you give us some guidelines which could be used in our daily studies in order to stay on the spiritual path and continue to move toward enlightenment?

Dr. Hora: Yes. Following are eleven points which, when daily contemplated and applied, will increase receptivity to divine grace and ensure progress on the spiritual path. These are parameters of progress, as taught at the New York Institute of Metapsychiatry.

1. Thou shalt have no other interests before the good of God, which is spiritual.

2. Take no thought for what should be of what should not be; seek ye first to know the good of God, which already is.

3. There is no interaction anywhere, there is only omniaction everywhere.

4. Yes is good, but no is also good.

5. God helps those who let Him.

6. If you know what, you know how.

7. Nothing comes into experience uninvited.

8. Problems are lessons designed for our edification.

9. Reality cannot be experienced or imagined; it can, however, be realized.

10. The understanding of what really is, abolishes all that seems to be.

11. Do not show your perils to unreceptive minds, for they will demean them.

READING LIST

1. Haas, W. S.: *The Destiny of the Mind, East and West.* Macmillan, New York, 1956.
2. Heidegger, M.: *Sein und Zeit.* Max Niemeyer Verlag, Tuebingen, 1953.
_____: *Was Heisst Denken.* Max Niemeyer Verlag, Tuebingen, 1954.
_____: *Gelassenheit.* Guenther Neske, Pfuellinge, 1959.
_____: *The Question of Being.* Twaine, New York, 1956.
3. Legge, J.: *The Texts of Taoism.* Julian Press, New York, 1959.
4. Ehrenwald, J.: *New Dimensions of Psychoanalysis.* Gruene & Stratton, New York, 1952.
5. Kelley, Th.: *A Testament of Devotion.* Harper & Row, New York, 1941.
6. James, W.: *The Varieties of Religious Experience.* Mentor, New York, 1961.
7. Fromm, E.: *The Art of Loving.* Harper & Row, New York, 1956.
8. Jung, C.G.: *The Undiscovered Self.* Mentor, New York, 1958.
_____: *Modern Man in Search of a Soul.* Harcourt, New York, 1933.
9. Tillich, P.: *Dynamics of Faith.* Harper & Row, New York, 1957.
10. Suzuki, D. T.: *Manual of Zen Buddhism.* Buddhist Society, Kyoto, 1935.
_____: *The Essence of Buddhism.* Buddhist Society, London, 1955.
11. Chun-Yuan Chang: *Self-Realization and the Inner Process of Peace.* Erahos Jahrbuch XXVII. Rein-Verlag, Zurich, 1959.
12. Bradley, F.H.: *Appearance and Reality.* Oxford University Press, London, 1955.
13. Hora, Th.: "The Epistemology of Love." *Journal of Existential Psychiatry,* Vol. II. No. 7. Winter 1962.
_____: "Religious Values in Illness and Health." *Journal of Religion and Health,* Vol. 2.,No.3., April 1963.
_____: "The Dynamism of Assumptions." *Topical Problems of Psychotherapy.* Vol.4. Karger, Basel-New York, 1963.
14. Merton, Th.: *Mystics and Zen Masters.* Farrar, Straus & Giroux, New York, 1966.
15. Berends, P. B.: *Whole Child-Whole Parent.* Harper's Magazine Press, New York, 1976.
16. Capra, F.: *The Tao of Physics.* Shamhala, Berkeley, 1975.
17. Tyrell, B. J.: *Christotherapy.* The Seabury Press, New York, 1975.
18. Graham, A. D.: *The End of Religion.* Harcourt Brace Jovanovich, New York-London, 1971.

INDEX

Index

Index

Salvation, 57, 197
Sanskrit, 37
Schizophrenic, 157
Scripture, 79
"Sea of mental garbage," 75, 76
Seder, 196
Self: abuse, 76; assurance, 204; confirmatory ideation, 11, 17, 113, 176, 182, 183, 184, 185, 205, 206, 224; confirmation, 79, 94, 135, 136, 152, 182, 206, 212; deception, 186; esteem, 107, 138, 204, 205, 206; existence, 191; identity, 82; indulgence, 15, 16, 17, 76, 103; pity, 112, 113, 135, 140, 183, 208; realization, 191; worth, 152
Selye, Hans, 146
Sensory perception, 158, 195
Sensualism, 51
Sermon on the Mount, 180
Sex, 116, 117, 121, 122, 123, 146; life, 201; therapy clinics, 210
Sexual: act, 109, 200; deviations, 203; intercourse, 123, 124; pleasure, 123, 124; power, 109
"Shouldlessness," 98, 160, 162, 165
Skepticism, 113
Social pressures, 21, 22
Soul, 29, 123, 178, 184
Spiritual: ambition, 152; basis, 207; commitment, 114; consciousness, 38, 11, 134, 161; counterfact, 57; counterpart, 124; discernment, 177; elite, 179; equivalent, 124, 204; evolution, 192; existence, 7; excellence, 179, 225; law, 42, 132; life, 33, 123; being(s), 72, 81, 96; liberation, 115; good, 187, 217; growth, 197; healing, 83; idea(s), 45, 80; identity, 95; journey, 159; joy, 60; manifestation, 106, 107; path, 123, 172, 179, 184, 196, 197, 230; perception, 120, 178; perspective, 101, 108, 131; point

of view, 101; progress, 90, 123, 192, 193, 195; qualities, 28; 164; reality, 61, 104, 151, 178, 192, 202; realization, 85, 115, 197; reflection(s), 126, 130; seers, 42, 177; solutions, 68, 206; strength, 202; standpoint, 193; substance, 103; truth, 99; values, 29, 30, 63, 99, 102, 120, 148, 187; wickedness, 172
Spontaneous remission, 83, 85
Stoicism, 129
Substance, 40, 100, 103, 104, 193
Suffism, 37
Suicide, 136
Summum bonum vitae, 52, 124
Supreme Intelligence, 221
Suzuki, Daïsitz, 120, 191
Symbolic structures, 77, 80, 81

T

Talmudists, 143
Taoism, 225; Taoist: literature, 219; wisdom, 122
Television, 91, 95, 97, 99, 115, 117, 179, 191, 208
Temptation, 86, 107, 125, 217
The Thinker, 26, 27, 28, 29, 82
Thinking: calculative, 26, 42, 166; cause-and-effect, 18, 73, 74, 150, 151, 197; conventional, 229; God-centered, 4, 5, 46; horizontal, 17, 18, 98, 139, 164, 226; malicious, 25; manipulative, 99, 102; operational, 99; parasitic, 106; right, 131; self-confirmatory, 17, 18, 113, 184; "should," 19, 33, 42, 217; spiritual, 48; wishful, 104
Transcendence, 1, 36, 123
Transformation of character, 1, 86
Transparency, 32, 33
Truth, 14, 39, 62, 67, 70, 79, 81, 88, 103, 112, 120, 127, 161, 174, 198,